To: The Hornbuckles
Merry Christmas 1985

Love Frank III

More
Footnotes

Dr. Gaston Foote

❈✤ *More* ✤❈

FOOTNOTES

by Gaston Foote

Published by
THE ARMAGH FOUNDATION

2401 Fountainview • Houston, Texas   77057

APPRECIATION

This book has been made possible through the courtesy of Houston Attorney, Donald E. Kilpatrick, who grew up at First Methodist Church, Fort Worth, Texas, where the author was minister for twenty-one years. And to his parents, Mr. and Mrs. Donald Lee Kilpatrick, who brought him.

FROM THE PUBLISHERS

For the past thirty-three years Gaston Foote has been writing a weekly column titled *Footnotes* for the *Fort Worth Star Telegram* in Fort Worth, Texas. From the more than sixteen hundred columns written, Dr. Foote has brought together a hundred and fifty of them in one cover. It has been our pleasure to be part of this enterprise.

Donald E. Kilpatrick
Houston, Texas

More
Footnotes

THEY SIGNED FOR US

Sometime ago I ran across a little book entitled, "They Signed For Us" which gave short, thumb-nailed sketches of the fifty-six signers of the Declaration of Independence. It gave me a thrill to know that every one of those men who signed the Declaration was a distinguished individual in his own right. Benjamin Franklin was the oldest (70) and Thomas Jefferson was the youngest (33). Do you remember the last line in the Declaration of Independence? It says: "And for the support of this declaration, with a firm reliance on the protection of Divine Providence, we mutually pledge to each other our lives, our fortunes and our sacred honor."

These gentlemen who signed for us paid a great price as underwriters of our liberty. As an example, Robert Morris, a shipping merchant, personally lost 150 ships during the war and received no compensation whatever.

I like the words of the pledge of allegiance to the flag and I believe, at least once a year, we ought to renew our gratitude for the freedoms we enjoy because of those who preceded us.

It is one nation, under God. These last two words were added to the pledge of allegiance. I'm especially grateful for that. Samuel Johnson said, "Patriotism is the last refuge of a scoundrel." Love of one's country must always be subservient to love of one's God. Hitler, Mussolini and all the dictators of the world have put their country before God—and wrecked their countries. God has only one code of ethics for all the nations on earth. Theft is theft if America is guilty just as other nations are guilty. Murder is murder here the same as anywhere else in the world. We can keep America strong only as we remember that ours is a nation under God.

It is one nation, under God, with liberty . . . Hosts of Americans have given their lives for the liberty that we enjoy. Freedom or liberty is a gift of God. We were born free. But in some areas of the world tyrannical men have robbed their fellowmen of their God-given freedom. Freedom is not the right to do what you want to do. This is anarchy. Freedom is the opportunity to do what you ought to do.

It is one nation, under God, with liberty and justice for all. The symbol of justice is a woman with a blindfold over her eyes and with scales in her hand. This does not mean that justice is blind; rather justice is impartial. We stand for equal opportunity of all our citizens. The day of equality of opportunity hasn't arrived yet, but we are making progress in that direction.

The fifty-six signers of the Declaration of Independence paid a great price for our freedom. On this 197th anniversary of their signing for us we ought to be signing it for ourselves. We joyfully salute those original signers of the Declaration of Independence as we stand in the singing of "God Bless America."

THE CHAPEL OF ALL FAITHS

It happened more than forty-three years ago during World War II. The Dorchester, a Liberty ship, had left New York harbor with sixteen hundred troops aboard bound for England.

It was after midnight when the lookout on the bridge spotted a German torpedo less than a hundred yards away. The captain turned the ship, but it was late. The torpedo struck amidships, blowing a hole some twenty feet in diameter. All alarms sounded simultaneously—then came the dreaded cry, "abandon ship."

All soldiers were told to put on their life belts and hasten to the upper deck. In a matter of minutes, dozens of lifeboats were being launched in the cold, angry waters off the Greenland coast. But some of the soldiers frantically reported that they had no life belts. Someone had made a terrible mistake . . . not enough belts to go around. Several teenagers, their faces white with fear, were frozen to the deck rail as they looked at the angry waters . . . without life belts, without hope.

Four chaplains on deck were helping men get into the lifeboats. When they saw the frantic young men without life belts, they buckled their own belts around the soldiers and shoved them into the last lifeboat to leave the ship. Those who lived to report the tragedy remembered the four chaplains putting their arms around each other and bowing their heads in prayer as the chilling waters engulfed them. The chaplains—a priest, a rabbi and two Protestant ministers—died so that others might live.

A grateful America did not forget them. There is a little chapel dedicated to their memory on the campus of Temple University in Philadelphia. It is called the Chapel of All Faiths. Three worship centers are built on an electric turntable. Push the button and you have a perfectly beautiful Protestant chapel. Push it again and you have a lively Catholic chapel. Push it the third time and you may worship in a Jewish synagogue.

Is this not what we mean when we talk about freedom of religion? I happen to be a Protestant by birth and conviction. But I would be miserable if I sought to get everyone to think like I think. I certainly hope no one on earth looks like I look. Why insist that they think like I think? It is for this reason that I never go to Philadelphia without spending a few moments in the Chapel of All Faiths.

THE FORWARD LOOK

Nature knew what she was doing when she put our eyes in the front of our heads instead of the back. To maintain the joy of living throughout the whole of life, we must have the forward look.

We must gratefully plan for tomorrow rather than nostalgically hang on to yesterday. Novelist Julia Ward Howe once was asked if it bothered her because she was growing older. Her sharp reply was, "No, because the sugar is in the bottom of the cup."

Hosts of our contemporaries seem to get a charge out of harking back to the good old days. I suppose it is because we remember the good times we had and forget the bad times. They never were as good as some people seem to think. But they hang on to yesterday and assume that all of the good things in life are behind them.

They are so sure that God is so disgusted with the universe he created, he is going to destroy it the day after tomorrow. I can hardly conceive of God as being so fickle. I know many people who make their lives miserable by looking backward with a sense of remorse and regret.

They lament the fact that they were poor, that they did not get a college education, that they were neither beautiful or handsome, that they should have married Jean instead of Jane or Jim instead of John.

In downtown Denver, Colorado, old Trinity Church has been opening its doors to passers by for almost a century. There is a gigantic light fixture in the center of the sanctuary with sixty-six light bulbs, evidently representing the sixty-six books in the Bible.

The minister's little son had memorized the names of the books and was going over the list while looking at the chandelier. Seeing that one of the lights was out, and utterly forgetting where he was he yelled, "Daddy, Lamentations is out."

Well, it ought to be out. Why cry over spilt milk? There is only one second that separates the past from the future and all the king's men cannot recall one second of the past.

Robert Browning spoke to our needs when he wrote, "Grow old along with me—The best is yet to be; the last of life for which the first was made."

To miss the truth of Browning is to miss the joy of living today. The secret of perpetual youth is a dynamic faith in the future. An outlook that does not help young people keep young all their lives has something wrong with it. It is unpardonable to grow old prematurely. Think of the ageless God of the universe.

BE THANKFUL FOR WHAT YOU HAVE

Tolstoy, famous Russian novelist, told the story of a large landowner who promised one of his servants all of the land he could run around between sunup and sundown. The servant, delighted with the prospect, set out the next day as soon as the sun peeped above the horizon, taking a fast gait due westward. Around ten o'clock he took a ninety-degree turn due south and ran until one. Again he made a ninety-degree turn due eastward. In midafternoon he started the homeward journey hoping to make it to the place from whence he started at sunup. But he was very tired; his feet dripped with blood, his eyes were bloodshot and his heart

beat like a machine gun. When the sun went down, too exhausted to walk, he was pulling himself on hands and knees along
the ground. The next morning, searchers found him miles from
his destination, dead from exhaustion.

Had this man been satisfied with less, he could have lived to
enjoy it. The story of this man's life is no isolated instance in
history. Countless millions of people never seem to be satisfied
with or grateful for what they have. Most of the millionaires I
know are still trying to make another dollar or two.

During the Thanksgiving season I renew my pledge to be
thankful for what I have and stop bothering about what is beyond
my reach. I have had about 355 good days of health every year
since I was born. I am not as young as I once was, but neither are
my neighbors. I cannot run as I once did and I seem to be using
the elevator rather than running up the steps. But I thank God
daily for the health I do have.

I don't have the influential friends some other people have.
Hollywood and Washington hostesses don't have my name on
their invitation lists. I can't begin my speeches with the "When I
was a guest at the White House" bit. Once I had tea with the
Queen of England at Buckingham Palace but I must admit that
two thousand other U.S. citizens were also present. But I do have
some wonderful salt-of-the-earth friends who believe in me and I
am going to spend a few minutes daily thanking God for them.

I don't have a mansion in which to live and my family isn't
famous for anything I ever heard of. But I am grateful for the roof
over my head and for my little family. Never again will I en-
viously peek into my rich neighbor's house. I'll just thank God for
what I have. This is my Thanksgiving prayer:

God, thou hast given much to me;
Give me one thing more—a thankful heart

CHROME-PLATED CHAOS

If you could choose the period in history in which your life would
be lived, what would you choose? When Columbus was discover-
ing new continents? When Washington was elected President of

the United States? When our great grandparents were moving westward in covered wagons in the gold rush?

If I had the choice I think I would choose today.

Undoubtedly, ours is a critical period in the history of mankind. We have lived through an era of almost unprecedented scientific advancement. There have been more changes in the past seventy-five years than in the previous two thousand.

A dozen of our fellow citizens have walked on the surface of the moon. We travel by plane faster than the speed of sound, talk to people on the opposite side of the globe and watch televised images of events around the world almost as they occur. We do things today that Jules Verne, in his most visionary moments, never imagined.

But what has become of all this progress? Our reaction has been wading through the bloodiest wars in history, developing enough explosive material to destroy every human being in the world fifty times over, having an unprecedented number of neurotics occupying every other bed in our hospitals, witnessing the breakdown of half the marital relationships in our homes, struggling with a frightening increase in crime and running up the largest liquor and dope bill in history.

Aldous Huxley has suggested that our technological progress enables us to move *backward* faster than ever before.

Surely we have an accumulated knowledge without wisdom. We have progressed intellectually but have fallen behind morally. We know all the answers except the important ones such as getting along with ourselves and our neighbors.

We have better houses but poorer homes. The mood in many of our homes is not unlike the husband who suggested to his wife that they go out and have a good time for once. Her reply was, "That was great, and if you get home before I do, leave the porch light on."

We have lost our way. A tourist, lost in the Burmese jungle, asked a native to lead him out. They proceeded in the underbrush until the native was hacking his own path. "Are you sure this is the way," asked the tourist. "There is no path," said the native "I am the way."

Since I think of this as God's world there is only one way out of the jungle . . . God's way.

HE IS ON MY LIST

In the old Gilbert and Sullivan operetta *The Mikado* there was a catchy tune, "I've Got A Little List." It was a list of those against whom the Emperor's son had a pet peeve. Tucked away in the dark corners of our minds I am sure we all have a similar list.

Do you remember the story of the woman who, bitten by a mad dog, got to the doctor too late? The doctor said, "I cannot help you; you are going mad." Whereupon she sat down and with pencil and paper began to write furiously, "Writing your will?" he asked, "No I'm making a list of the people I'm going to bite."

Well, heading my list is the fellow who is always telling his friends about a neat little deal where he is sure they can make at least a million bucks. It seems like I have met this man somewhere before.

Running a close second is the fellow hypnotized by the sound of his own voice, who insists on telling you a long-winded story in a thousand pointed words when a maximum of ten words would have been better. While you listen respectfully, the lights change a dozen times, the parking meter flashes red, the luncheon soup gets cold and another payment comes due on your car. Furthermore, you heard the story back when you were a child.

Even preachers admit that they have their secret peeve lists. One is the highly loquacious church member who backs you up in a corner and recalls, with warm enthusiasm and much gesticulation, how much better off the church was when Dr. Demosthenes was pastor. The church was always full with more than a thousand in attendance. Never mind the official records indicating an average attendance of 407. Who cares about the facts?

I'm reminded of the dear little lady who came up after one of my sermons and wistfully remarked, "Preaching is not what it used to be." Then she added, "And it never was."

Then there is brother E. Pluribus Unum who has been a pillar in the church for fifty years. He believes in pledging and paying to the church. But he follows the Old Testament admonition to "remove not the ancient landmarks" which includes his pledge of a dollar a week. Despite inflation and high water, he will be there with a dollar every Sunday.

Methinks by now I am on your list. Never mind, I'll quit. Remember that an optimist is a man who reaches for his hat when the preacher says, "Now in conclusion . . ."

WHOM THE GODS DESTROY . . .

In the year 1828 Noah Webster published his first dictionary of the English language. It included 12,000 words and 44,000 definitions. One of the definitions was that of a proverb, which he defined as "an enigmatical saying in which a profound truth is cloaked."

Historians generally agree that you can sum up the teachings of history by the proverbs which the sages of the ages have written.

One of those proverbs is "Whom the gods would destroy they first make mad." Regardless of who wrote it, it seems to be loaded with profound truth.

Who do you suppose is the most deeply hated person in the twentieth century? My guess is Adolf Hitler. As you may know, Hitler grew up a poor boy, intensely proud of his German blood, disgustingly hateful of Jewish blood.

One of the great days in his life was when he was appointed chancellor in 1933. His first act was to outlaw all rival political parties. He sent his opponents to concentration camps, where many of them died from torture and starvation.

Jewish mothers with babes in arms were enticed to follow Hitler's guides, who promised food and shelter but gave them poison gas and death. The holocaust of Adolf Hitler is sufficient evidence of the truth of the proverb "Whom the gods would destroy they first make mad."

He and his friend Eva Braun drank the potion snuffing out their lives.

There is, however, a more recent evidence of the truth of this proverb. A young man by the name of James Jones who lived in a small town in east Indiana told his rather impoverished parents that he wanted to be a preacher.

He asked for, and was admitted into, the ministry of one of our Protestant denominations. In the course of time he became a fascinating orator, possessing what some people might call hypnotic ability.

He established an independent church in the northern area of San Francisco. He cultivated and won the hearts of the political and religious leaders of the city. He opened the doors of this church to the poor, the homeless, the destitute.

But evidently his success went to his head. He became a dictator to his congregation, demanding absolute obedience. When outside opposition became unbearable, he moved his entire congregation to Guyana, South America.

When he threatened to move to Russia, the entire world turned against him. So he determined to make martyrs of his group. With enough poison to destroy every one of them, he begged them to sacrifice their lives for his cause.

Nine hundred and seventeen men, women and children drank with him the poison that snuffed out their lives. "Whom the gods would destroy they first make mad."

IF I WERE THE DEVIL . . .

If I were the devil . . .

I would begin a whispering campaign telling all the young people in the world what the serpent whispered to Eve, "Do your own thing, you are young only once in your life." I would tell them that the Bible is a myth and convince them that man created God rather than that God created man . . . just like the communists teach it. I would tell them that hard work simply shortens their lives; if they wish to enjoy their youthful years to the fullest they must go to all the cocktail and pot parties in the Metroplex unless they are too drunk to walk.

If I were the devil . . .

I would insist that no teacher had the right to mention his or her religious faith in any fashion whatever. I would evict God from the schoolhouse, the courthouse and the houses of Congress.

If I were the devil . . .

I would grant pardons to terrorists and send all conscientious objectors to the penitentiary for life. I would tip the scales of justice in favor of the rich regardless of the methods they might have used in gathering their fortunes. I would have no sympathy for the poor and the jobless. If they could not find work for themselves, let them and their children starve.

If I were the devil . . .

I would throw the government into backruptcy by appropriating vast sums of money for national defense and nothing for the impoverished multitudes and near-starving at home. I would scare people into believing that there is a subversive organization in every dark corner of the world waiting for a government takeover.

If I were the devil . . .

I would make the symbol of Christmas a bottle of liquor and the symbol of Easter a dyed hen egg.

If I were the devil . . .

I would just keep on doing what the devil seems to have been doing since the days of Adam and Eve. I hear that Adam still grumbles because, when he was asleep, God took a rib out of his side and made his sidekick—Eve.

LIES THAT BLIND

More realistic in our day than the "ties that bind" are the "lies that blind." The trouble with a lie is that one lie calls for two more. It is not without reason that, embedded in the Ten Commandments is the solemn warning "Thou shalt not bear false witness."

The greatest crimes of history were perpetrated by lies. It was a lie that brought about the crucifixion of Christ. His enemies said he was a winebibber, a blasphemer, a hypocrite. The first wholesale slaughter of Christians was the result of a lie. Because Nero spread the lie that the Christians were responsible for the burning of Rome, hundreds of them were murdered in the streets.

There are many modern methods of lying. We can lie by insinuation. Two women were discussing a third person who happened to be a charming, intelligent social leader. One of them asked, "Do you suppose she is straight?" When the name of a successful business man came up someone asked, "Do you think he made his money honestly?"

We can lie by silence. If a man is being falsely accused in my presence, I have a responsibility to speak, lest I become a party to the lie. Robert Louis Stevenson said, "A man can sit in a room for hours and not open his mouth and come out of that room a disloyal friend or a vile calumniator."

Probably the most popular method of lying is by half-truth. Let me illustrate. Two men, in strict secrecy, carefully made plans to catch another man and destroy him. They chased him over several states and, finally, by conniving and wire tapping, surprised him when he slept, caught him and shot him. Now every word of that statement is true . . . but only a half-truth. The two men were officers of the law tracking down a triple murderer and had to shoot him in self-defense. You see how important the whole truth is?

There is no virtue more highly prized than telling the truth. Tennyson said of the duke of Wellington, "He never sold the truth to serve the hour." The bard of Avon, William Shakespeare, said: "This above all to thine own self be true. And it must follow, as the night the day, thou canst not be false to any man."

PRAYER CHANGES PEOPLE

Years ago I attended a mass meeting where a world-famous evangelist was speaking. Across the gigantic stage there was a sign which read: "Prayer changes things." Through the years I have had some questions about that sign.

I really don't believe that prayer changes things. I love growing plants in my home but I have never resorted to the method of keeping them alive through prayer. If I really love them enough I will take care of them without bothering God about their health.

Let me hasten to say that I do believe that prayer changes people who pray. To put it simply, prayer is the practice of the presence of God. It is the exposure of the soul to the highest that we know. Made in God's likeness, through prayer we communicate with our Maker.

Once a spiritual adviser said to Madame Guyon, the eighteenth-century mystic: "Madame, you are seeking without that which you already have within you. Accustom yourself to seek God in your own heart and you will find Him."

God is not only in the hereafter, He is in the here now. He is still creating the world according to His plans and is enlisting His children to help Him. And it is through prayer that we learn to help Him in His purposes.

Prayer releases power in the person who prays. Dr. Alexis Carrel, physician and scientist, says: "Prayer is the most powerful form of energy that can be generated. Its influence on the human mind is as demonstrable as that of the secreting glands of the body. I have seen men, after all therapy has failed, lifted out of disease and melancholy by the supreme effort of prayer."

Prayer is not a good luck charm, not a magic wand to pull rabbits out of hats, not a sleight-of-hand performance to evade our personal responsibilities. Prayer is a workable experience wherein we enlist the cooperation of the Creator in our day to day living. Prayer gives us inner peace in a world of panic, calm in a world of calamity, hope in a world of despair.

Dr. Harry Fosdick, outstanding pulpit divine in New York City a generation ago, told the story of a fisherman and his two sons who were caught off the New England coast in a small craft while a storm was raging.

The father, seeing that his sons were almost paralyzed by fear, said to them: "Boys, there is a little mother over there on the coast of New England who is on her knees praying for our safe return home tonight. To the oars, boys, let's help her get those prayers answered."

LEGEND OF THREE TREES

Some two thousand years ago, so the legend goes, there were three trees growing on the slope of a mountain overlooking the Jordan river. They were discussing their hopes for the future.

One of the trees wanted to be cut down, hauled to a lumber yard and be made into beautiful panels for the temple of worship.

The second tree had a dream of being made into a sleek sailing ship giving pleasure to those crossing the Mediterranean Sea.

The third tree lifted its branches and prayed to remain in its place and grow heavenward so that men might lift their eyes upward and think of God.

But when the axe men came, all the trees were cut down. The first tree, which sought to be paneling in the temple, was used to build a stable in the town of Bethlehem, where donkeys munched the hay.

The second tree, far from being a sailing vessel on the Mediterranean, became a fishing boat on the sea of Galilee, enduring the despair of being filled daily with smelly fish.

The third tree finally was cut down and hauled into Jerusalem where it was shaped into three crosses, instruments of death for common criminals.

The three trees could scarcely bear the shame of such indignities.

We obviously know the rest of the story.

The first tree became the stable where a woman named Mary gave birth to a little boy whose name was Jesus.

The second tree became the fishing boat from which the Son of God spoke to the multitudes.

And from one of the crosses made from the third tree, we are reminded that this human-divine father is the supreme architect of the universe and whose name is love.

"For God so loved the world. . . ." On this Christmas season we feel that we constantly can see God walking down the stairway of heaven with a baby in his arms.

DOES GOD REALLY LAUGH?

In Psalm 2:4 we find this quotation: "God who sits in the heavens laughs." Though I have been in the ministry almost 60 years, I have never preached on that text. But if the psalmist thinks that God laughs, we are inclined to believe a hearty laugh now and then is a perfectly normal way to live.

Someone has said: "Laugh and the world laughs with you/ Weep and you weep alone/ For this sad old earth has to borrow its mirth/ But has trouble enough of its own."

One of Billy Graham's cherished stories is that about a minister who gave a sermon on the dignity of work. But he said in the sermon, "You don't have to work every day since, because of Moses, you have Saturday off and, because of Jesus, you have Sunday off. Isn't that wonderful?"

"Sure is," said a voice from the back pew, "five more Jewish boys like that and we would never have to work at all."

Another minister, in concluding his sermon on the evils of alcohol, said, "If I had my way I would gather up all the liquor in the country and dump it in the river. Now let us bow our heads for the closing hymn." Whereupon, the choir director led the congregation in singing, *Shall we gather at the river?*

"Today I want to preach to you about liars," said a minister. "How many of you have read the 29th chapter of Matthew?" About half the people in the church raised their hands. "You are the ones I want to talk to," said the minister. "There is no 29th chapter of Matthew."

"Does your father ever preach the same sermons twice?" someone asked the minister's 10-year-old son. "He sure does," said the son, "But he hollers in different places."

On their way home from church the young couple discussed the minister's message. The wife said, "I didn't think he put enough fire into his sermon." The husband replied, "In my opinion, he didn't put enough of his sermon into the fire."

One Saturday after a Notre Dame football game, one of the players went to a confessional booth and told the priest some of the things that had transpired during the game:

"I deliberately kicked an opponent on his shins," said the player. "Awful," said the priest.

"I stepped on his hand with my cleats," said the player. "Terrible, terrible," said the priest.

"I hit him in the mouth and knocked out two of his teeth," said the penitent. "Absolutely unforgivable," said the priest, who then asked, "Who were you playing?"

"Southern Methodist University," said the player. "Oh well, boys will be boys," said the priest.

A Protestant minister planned to preside at a wedding ceremony when he discovered that his watch was slow and he was going to be late. He hastily put on his black robe and white stole, put his wife in the car, stepped on the gas and promptly ran a red light.

The policeman who stopped him said, "Father, you must promise to slow down or I shall give you a ticket." After the minister humbly promised and thanked the officer, his wife said, "Honey, you are flying under false colors. That officer thinks you are a priest." He replied, "It doesn't really matter who he thinks I am; it is who he thinks you are that bothers me."

TO TELL THE TRUTH

Sometime ago I saw a plaque hanging on the office wall of a leading business man in our city. It was called the Four Way Test— of things we think, say or do. The first test was, "Is It the Truth?"

Did it ever occur to you how different the atmosphere would be if we honestly would ask ourselves, "Is it the truth?"

Lord Tennyson said of the duke of Wellington, "He never sold the truth to serve the hour." Do we?

The truth is so important that it is written in the earliest of the Commandments of God; "Thou shalt not bear false witness."

Telling the truth is the cornerstone of enduring character.

Failure to tell the truth, lying, has perpetrated the greatest crimes in history. Jesus was crucified because of a lie. His enemies said He was a wine-bibber, a blasphemer, a hypocrite.

The latest crime of genocide, the slaughter of five million Jews in Germany under Hitler, was made possible by lies about the Jewish people living in their midst.

We can lie by insinuation. "Have you heard that Mr. Blank is a card-carrying Communist?" "Did he make his money honestly?" "Is he a wife beater?"

We can lie by half truths. "Two men from Washington cornered a man in the mountains of New Mexico, spied on him, cornered him and shot him to death." Now every word of that statement is true. But only a half truth. The two men who gave chase were federal officers in pursuit of a desperado. When they sought to arrest him they had to shoot him in self-defense.

We can lie by being perfectly silent. If we do not speak up in behalf of some good man who is being demeaned or vilified in our presence we consent to his unjust condemnation simply by silence.

We can lie by repeating a lie. Most of us call it gossip.

To tell the truth is not a program in a TV guide. It is a test of character.

PRAYING HANDS SYMBOLIZES LOVE

In a European art gallery there is a famous picture called *Praying Hands*. Behind this painting is a beautiful story.

Somewhere around the turn of the fourteenth century, two young men from Nuremburg, Germany, both planned to study art. But they were both poor and found it impossible to work as day laborers and study art at the same time. So the older of the two said to his friend that he would work and provide food and lodging for the two of them, allowing the younger, Albrecht Durer, to be free to study art in earnest. Later, they would exchange places and the older man would pursue his career in art.

The agreement made, Durer studied art while his friend worked as a stonemason to provide food and shelter for both men. And when Durer had sold his first painting, he insisted that he and his partner change places and he would provide the food and lodging.

So his friend took up the brush and began to paint.

But something terrible had happened while Durer had studied. His friend's hands, having been dedicated to hard labor, were stiff, the joints enlarged, and he realized that his ability to become an artist had gone forever.

When Durer learned what happened to his friend he was filled with great sorrow. Coming home earlier than usual one day Durer heard the voice of his friend in prayer and saw his friend's gnarled hands lifted above his head. Durer said to himself, "I cannot give back the lost skill of those hands which have sacrificed for me. But I will paint those hands as they are now, folded in prayer, and the world will know of my deep appreciation of such a noble and unselfish friend."

Durer became a distinguished painter for European kings. But those rough hands with broken fingernails and enlarged joints remains one of the most moving pictures I have ever seen.

Have we become so self-centered as to forget the devoted hands of our mothers and fathers who labored so diligently for our welfare? Dare we ignore the supreme sacrifices of those in our armed services who have given their lives that we might enjoy our freedoms? It's about time we stopped bewailing our fate and began counting our blessings.

OUR GREATEST GIFT

At a Rotary Club meeting sometime ago, I was privileged to hear a magnificent, moving address. The speaker was a Russian Jew who had only recently emigrated from the land of his birth. He was an important citizen in the Soviet Union, having been a teacher in a school for the training of computer experts.

But out of a clear sky and to his utter amazement, he had been fired from his position as a teacher and was, without warning, assigned to an inferior job as a day laborer in a factory.

The reason for his being fired was a letter written by one of the students accusing him of being disloyal to the government. There was no evidence given for the accusation; no questions were asked, no trial took place. He was simply dismissed without warning.

Being of Jewish blood, he asked for the privilege of being exported to Israel. Since he did not care to remain in Israel, he came to Waco, where he is employed by the Police Department working with computers.

I wish all of America could have heard this new immigrant's address. He said there were only two choices for the people in the Soviet Union. . . . either obey the orders sent down from the bosses or get out of the country.

Because he is Jewish he was able to leave. Can you imagine millions of people living in this kind of an environment? Living in constant fear of having some thought contradictory to the pronounced opinion of heads of government? And with no recourse in a court of justice?

It is extremely important for us to remember that, as we celebrate the occasion of the birth of our nation, freedom is positively the most precious asset the United States has to offer.

We did not achieve our freedom as a nation in 1776 by winning a war with England. We were born free . . . by the authority of Almighty God. And may God have pity upon us if we ever lose the freedom to think, to speak, to work, to worship, and to choose.

RELIGIOUS CONFLICTS

When religion becomes a rallying cry for conflict, fighting becomes all the more bitter and peacemaking practically impossible.

Some 40 years ago, Great Britain offered independence to India and Nehru became the first prime minister. Almost immediately, fighting broke out between the two largest religious groups, the Hindus and the Moslems.

Unfortunately, they have been at it ever since. Literally millions of Indians have died in the never-ending struggle. And all of it is in the name of religion.

One leader told his followers that it was their "religious duty to send their opponents to hell by destroying them." One can imagine that the road to hell is paved with hate in the name of religion.

The carnage in India and elsewhere is not only between Hindus and Moslems but between the Moslem brothers. Ayatollah Khomeini in Iran and his Shiite Moslem followers have, for the last five years, been in a death struggle against other Moslems, the Sunnis in Iraq. I don't know what the devil looks like but I have the feeling that Khomeini looks somewhat like him. He sends thousands of teenagers into battle promising them a guaranteed trip to heaven in case they get killed. Thoughtful of him, is it not? Heaven is my home, too, but I am not particularly homesick.

It was Khomeini who plotted the assassination of President Sadat in Egypt, so historians tell us. Someone has said that hell is . . . other people. And so it seems.

The plague of religious wars throughout the world is phenomenal. Our American Marines sought to help the Lebanese in their difficulties, but those difficulties remain.

The wearing of a Christian cross or an Islamic crescent in the wrong Beirut neighborhood is an invitation to murder.

And, not unlike Beirut, there is Belfast. Northern Ireland is an area of bitter strife between Protestants and Catholics. Thousands of people have been injured or killed within the last decade. Protestant and Catholic children have their separate schools and grow up hating one another.

The more we read about world-wide religious wars, the more we become sickened by the situation. And the more grateful we are for the good old U.S. of A. Our forefathers made no mistake when they made individual freedom the cornerstone of our commonwealth.

On the block where we live, there are 10 homes with typical American families. There are at least three different religions represented . . . Protestant, Catholic and Jewish . . . and possibly an agnostic or two. So what? We like it this way.

THE WEALTH OF THE COMMUNITY—PEOPLE

Oliver Goldsmith, the eighteenth-century poet and novelist, once wrote:

Ill fares the land,
To hastening ills a prey,
Whose wealth accumulates
And men decay.

It would be interesting to examine the meaning of this two-hundred-year-old phrase in light of what is happening in the United States today. Goldsmith evidently questioned the philosophy of his beloved England, whose chief interest seemed to have been the wealth of the nation rather than the well-being of the people, rich and poor, within the nation.

There is something wrong with the United States when twelve million people roam the streets looking for jobs that are not available; when good people, through no fault of their own, spend hours in breadlines to keep body and soul together.

In Goldsmith's day, honest hardworking people "decayed" because they gradually lost hope. It could happen to us here.

President Reagan has assumed, I believe honestly, that what is good for the rich will trickle down to help the poor. But it hasn't turned out that way, save from an elder Rockefeller to younger one.

America, boasting about its democratic ways, must be judged by the way it treats its minority groups. And these people are not being given a fair shake. Food stamps were taken away from some people who desperately needed them, simply because of a few grafters who muddied the water.

An inferior lunch was given poor children in our public schools because some people abused the privilege. Government loans to ambitious young people were curtailed because it was felt we needed additional neutron bombs.

Oliver Goldsmith was right. England, and every other country is wrong when it puts wealth ahead of people. A nation's people are the most important element in any community. Demean the people, especially the impoverished, and you ultimately destroy them. Dignify them, all of them, the rich and the poor, the strong and the weak, the blacks and the whites, and they rise to greater heights of expectancy. This is inevitably true because we were all created in the image of the Eternal.

NO SECOND-HAND FAITH

On the steps of the church a few Sundays ago I greeted a visitor who said she was a Presbyterian. With a twinkle in my eye, I facetiously asked, "Why aren't you a Methodist?" She replied, "My grandfather was a Presbyterian minister, my father was a Presbyterian minister, so naturally I am a Presbyterian."

Hoping to get in the last good lick and, still with a twinkle in my eye, I said, "Then, if your grandfather had been an idiot and your father had been an idiot, what would you have been?" She spoke in a calm, measured tone, saying, "I understand what you mean. Under those circumstances I suppose I would have been a Methodist."

Which was not exactly what I had in mind.

On a deeper level, most of us are what we are, not altogether by conviction, but also by inheritance. Our political affiliations are usually determined by the political alliances of our parents. As a rule, Democrats beget Democrats, Republicans beget Republicans, independents beget independents. The slant toward liberalism or conservatism is not necessarily by conviction but by inheritance.

Our prejudices are usually the result of our parents. As the song in *South Pacific* has it: "You've got to be taught to hate." A little baby is born with the prejudice of the tribe tattooed on its skin. It is always a good idea to take our prejudices out in the open sunlight and carefully examine them in the light of reason.

Some people assume that religion is simply the result of the heritage received from our parents. But the truth is, there is no such thing as a second-hand faith. We can sing the "Faith of our Fathers" until we are blue in the face but we can never capture that faith until it becomes completely our own. Man cannot appropriate the God of his ancestors. One's religion is a spiritual experience, not simply an intellectual concept. Man doesn't inherit God; if he knows Him he experiences Him. An honest agnostic asked a minister how he knew there was a God. The minister replied, "Because I talked to Him a few minutes ago."

YOU CAN TAKE IT WITH YOU

Bob Hope used to kid his buddy Bing Crosby for singing, "There's a gold mine in the sky." He said that while Bing knew he could not take his money with him when he passed on, he could "shoot it up there" and pick it up en route.

In a real sense, however, one can take significant elements of this life into the unknowable future. Consider, for instance, the fact that we can so invest our time today that we can live tomorrow. We can't hoard time; it is obviously impossible for us to save time. But we can invest it in opportunities for service to others in such a way that those minutes we have used as good Samaritans will live forever in other lives.

Along about the turn of the century a young man from a Christian mission felt led to go out and talk to a Chicago Cub baseball player about surrendering his life to Christ.

The name of the ball player? It was Billy Sunday (the Billy Graham of his day) whose preaching brought thousands of others to a commitment to the Christian faith. Surely this unknown disciple knew how to invest the priceless gift of time into eternity.

Furthermore, we can so invest our talents that our influence will live forever.

In a small West Texas town there was a Sunday school teacher of a group of twelve- and thirteen-year-old boys. The teacher was not particularly brilliant, but he was faithful and devoted to every boy in the group. From that class came four young men who subsequently committed their lives to the Christian ministry. I remember that man well for I was one of those four young men. Surely the talents of that Sunday school teacher are still alive.

Finally, contrary to public opinion, we can take money with us if we invest it properly. Some years ago I visited on the campus of a small Christian college in Japan. Graduates of that school are known in all sections of that island empire. The funds to establish and endow the college were given by a U.S. philanthropist, A. A. Hyde, the Mentholatum king, who passed away almost a century ago. Did I say passed away?

Indeed, this is the essence of Christian stewardship—taking the things you can't keep (time, talent, treasure) and investing them in the things you can't lose. And if there is a gold mine in the sky, it will be because you put it there.

CROSS-EYED RELIGION

People whose eyes are crossed appear to be looking at one thing and actually seeing another. The Apostle Peter, in his moments of weakness, seemed to be so afflicted in his religious outlook.

When he and James and John were on the mount of transfiguration with the Lord and Jesus' "garments became white as light," Peter said, "Lord it is well that we are here; let us build three tabernacles."

But Jesus led them down into the valley where there were suffering people in need of healing. Peter, in the face of human need, wanted to stay on the mountain top for a religious good time.

Not infrequently the local church becomes too local. It concerns itself only with its own four walls and overlooks the physical and spiritual impoverishment of helpless and hopeless people in the neighborhood.

In another instance, Jesus told his disciples he was to go to Jerusalem, possibly to be crucified. Peter took Jesus to one side and said, "This will never happen to you." Peter could see only the tragedies of crucifixion, not the redemption through love on the cross.

Ask someone to teach a Sunday School class of thirteen-year-olds and all they see is the irksome task of discipline and constant preparation, overlooking the joy of making an indelible contribution on a growing youngster. The church that will not bleed cannot bless; if it will not serve it cannot save.

Again, Peter asked Jesus which one of the disciples might possibly betray him. Jesus said "What is that to thee? Follow thou me." Peter, instead of being concerned with his own loyalty, was seeking to know the real betrayer.

Cross-eyed religion gets us nowhere. Only the man who looks with steady eyes into his own life and in the eyes of the master becomes a transformed person.

ABE LINCOLN'S FAITH

It is common knowledge that Abraham Lincoln, whose birthday

we celebrate, was not a member of any church. But it ought to be said in the same breath that he was one of the most dedicated persons in the history of the United States.

Because of this apparent ambivalence in his life, he was one of the most beloved, and most hated Presidents in American history. Newspapers in both the North and South, almost without exception, vilified him in the most abusive and slanderous language at their command.

He was referred to as an atheist, agnostic, Christ killer, gorilla, country greenhorn, obscene clown, the baboon president and more.

But the sober reflections of history indicate an entirely different person against the backdrop of the passing years. He was deeply devoted to his mother and never seemed to get away from the truths he learned at his mother's knee. He regularly read the Scriptures.

As a youth he had few books, but the Bible was the one he prized most. He could quote many of the most meaningful passages in the Bible from memory. One day he said concerning it, "This book is the best gift God has given to man. All the good the Savior brought to the world was communicated through this book. Without it we could not know right from wrong."

Lincoln believed in divine leadership. Here are his words when he left Springfield, Ill., to assume the presidency: "I leave now, not knowing when, or whether ever I shall return, with a task before me greater than that which rested on the shoulders of Washington. With the assistance of Divine Providence, who always attended him, I cannot fail. Trusting in Him can go with me and yet remain with you, let us confidently hope that all will be well."

In all probability Lincoln's most familiar words for the average American are found in his "Gettysburg Address." Here is the bottom line: Let us "here highly resolve that these dead shall not have died in vain; that this nation, under God, shall have a new birth of freedom, and that government of the people, by the people, and for the people, shall not perish from the earth."

I don't know why Lincoln didn't belong to a church. But I am convinced he did belong to that larger fellowship where the people of God are considered the most important element in the world.

It is not the church to which I belong nor the creed to which I subscribe that is most important; it is my reverence for and appreciation of God's children about me, regardless of race, creed or color, that matters.

DON'T CUT OFF THE BUTTONS

Obviously, private enterprise is alive and well in the United States in as much as I see garage sales advertised all around the neighborhood. Concerning them, a deservedly unknown poet has written: "A garage sale by any other name, sells lots of junk that's all the same."

But since one man's dud is another man's fortune, garage sales have evidently moved in for good. As the saying goes, old bargains never die. They are merely reincarnated in another man's carport.

Clothes are the stock in trade of most all garage sales. One heavily upholstered woman remarked, "I enjoy giving away my extra clothing to charity but I usually cut off the buttons in case I might need them later."

If, as James Russell Lowell reminds us, "the gift without the giver is bare," It would seem that a coat without the buttons in the dead of winter would be bare indeed.

Ministers are well aware of Mr. Gotrocks on Plush Avenue who is always willing to make a liberal contribution to the church, provided he is allowed to dictate to the official board exactly how every penny must be spent. All he wants is the right to run the church all by himself. Snip, snip. A case of giving a coat and cutting off the buttons.

There are many bargain hunters among us who wish to contribute a hundred dollars providing they can get two hundred dollars' worth of publicity out of it. These gifts are made with the disdainful air of patronage.

It is looking down one's nose at the socially unwashed with the feeling of "Oh, did the Lord make you too?" That snips off the buttons no matter the size of the gift.

Here are some quotes from the Bible: "Beware of practicing your piety before men in order to be seen by them. When you give alms, sound no trumpet as do the hypocrites . . . give alms in secret so your Father in secret may reward you."

In Jesus' day the winner of the Nobel Prize for philanthropy was the Good Samaritan. He left all the buttons on the coat and sent along an extra set. On the tomb of an unknown soldier in Europe is this carving: "He gave his all and forgot to sign his name."

GRACE NOTES ADD THE SPICE

I often find myself writing about things I know little about. Since I know little about music I am going to write about grace notes.

I cannot tell the difference between a flock of grace notes in flight and a herd of counterpoint. Grace notes are little bevies of flags and dots atop the musical staff which, though not essential to the melody, add enormously to the attractiveness of the music. Grace notes in life are not essential in the pursuit of our duties but they add enormously to the joy of living.

In one of his plays, Shakespeare has Iago to say of Desdemona: "She holds it a vice in her goodness not to do more than that which is required." Desdemona simply adds grace notes in her relationship with those about her.

Jesus said it like this: "Whoever compels you to go with him one mile, go with him two." The great joys in life come, not from the first mile of compulsion, but from the second mile of privilege. Stern voices of duty have no grace notes. They are like taking a cold shower at 6 a.m.

Consider the day's work. People who love their work do not watch the clock. Artists make play out of their work because they strive for perfection. Chopin wrote musical scores over and over as many as a hundred times, not because the first writing was unacceptable to the public, but because the first 99 writings were unacceptable to Chopin. Work without grace notes sprinkled around is sheer drudgery.

Consider marriage, if you haven't already. Marriage without grace notes is a dreadfully long journey. To make the marital relationship a consuming joy, there must be a generous supply of tuneful grace notes . . . where partners insist on doing more than that which is required. Christopher Morley once said "the plural of spouse is spice." True . . . spice is a stimulating seasoning for a successful marriage.

Our shallowness in conversation is largely due to the scarcity of grace notes. Some people have nothing more to talk about than the weather . . . or the government. One of our contemporary sages remarked, "It is not what is on the table that counts, but what is on the chairs." When conversations degenerate to "what channel does the prize fight come in on" there is desperate need for some lifesaving grace notes.

THE MOST FAMOUS ROAD

Probably the most famous road in the world is the one from Jerusalem to Jericho, a distance of some twenty-two miles. The road has been made famous because of Jesus' story of the Good Samaritan. A lawyer asked Him the pointed question, "Who is my neighbor?" Jesus told this simple story to illustrate what he meant by being a good neighbor.

There are three principal participants in the story: the robber, the priest and Levite—and the good Samaritan. Each of the participants had a distinctive philosophy of life, not at all unlike the philosophy of men in our day.

The philosophy of the robber was, "What is thine is mine— I'll take it." When he overtook the lone traveler on the road he accosted him, robbed him and left him half dead by the roadside. It is shocking to think that there are some eight million people in the United States who make their living by breaking the law of the land. Furthermore, the costs of crime are outrageous, amounting to more than the total bill for public education of our youth.

The philosophy of the priest and Levite was, "What is mine is mine—I'll keep it." I don't suppose either the priest or Levite had much money in their pockets since I haven't seen too many rich priests or preachers in my day. But, despite the obvious need of the man who was bleeding in the ditch, they both passed by on the other side. I am sure they had legitimate excuses for being in a hurry. But, generally speaking, anyone who doesn't have time to render first aid when a man is in serious trouble is not a good neighbor.

The philosophy of the good Samaritan was, "What is mine is thine—I'll share it." But let the Bible speak: "A Samaritan came to where he was and had compassion on him and bound up his wounds, pouring in oil and wine; then he set him on his own beast and brought him to an inn and took care of him." Then Jesus asked the lawyer, "Which of these three do you think proved neighbor to the man who fell among the robbers?" The lawyer answered correctly, "The one who showed mercy."

At the moment literally thousands of people in Tarrant County are spending their time and money to support the many agencies of the United Way that we might be good neighbors to those less fortunate than ourselves. So when a volunteer worker calls on you, you'll be a good neighbor, won't you? You will be glad you did—and so will those you help!

'UNBAPTIZED ARMS'

Ivan the Terrible was the first ruler of Russia to crown himself Czar. He was given that descriptive name because of his ruthless, tyranical rule over his people for fifty-one bloody years, from 1533 to 1584. For example, he killed his only son in a fit of anger.

Ivan was so busy fighting the neighboring states that he did not marry until he was middle aged. When his subjects suggested that he marry, he dispatched a retinue of servants to find the most beautiful girl of royal blood in the civilized world.

They found her in Athens, Greece. Her name was Sophia, daughter of the King of Greece. When Ivan asked the King for his daughter's hand, the King made him promise to join the Greek Orthodox Church.

Ivan obviously wanted to make a big affair of the wedding, so he went to Athens accompanied by five hundred of his best soldiers. They in turn volunteered to join the church with him.

When the priests outlined the articles of confession to the soldiers they agreed to all of them save one. This article stated that if they joined the church they could not be professional soldiers. They asked themselves: "How can we join the church and remain in the army at the same time"?

They came up with the following plan: All five hundred of them, together with five hundred priests, would march in the water at the same time. But before each priest took his candidate under water, each soldier grabbed his sword, lifted it in the air and was baptized save for his fighting arm and gleaming sword.

Witnesses to the baptisms saw 500 dry arms and shining swords high above the waters. They were saying they would join the church with their bodies but their fighting arms would remain in possession of the state.

This situation epitomizes the church today. We have too many unbaptized arms. We make too many reservations when we join the church. We yield to God only in part. The curse of the hour is the curse of partial surrender.

This does not mean we expect to achieve perfection. It should mean complete commitment to the ways of the Kingdom of God, who can do a lot with ordinary people like us. But he has to have all of us there is.

ARCHIE BUNKER'S GOD

"In the beginning, Archie Bunker created God in his own image. In his own image created He him." Thus Spencer Marsh, author of "God, Men and Archie Bunker" tells the story of one of the most durable characters in TV history. It sounds a bit weird, like the clay forming the potter, but the difference between this statement and the Genesis account is that God and Archie have changed places.

Traditionally God made men in his own image. In this instance the man made God in his own image.

Archie is not unique in this respect. We are all inclined to reject the traditional God of revelation and fashion a God with whom we can live more comfortably. We in America are inclined to touch up our image of God so he will look somewhat like Uncle Sam.

The poor man feels that God is particularly sensitive to the needs of the impoverished. The hard working hardhat fashions for himself a hardhat God. The driving executive worships an executive God. The militant has a militant God, always at the ready to destroy his enemies.

Archie's God has all the weaknesses of Archie. In the same breath he speaks of God as dropping the bomb on Hiroshima and those useless "pink Commie Chinks." He undertakes to rewrite the Bible. He says, "God made for every one the same religion— Christian. That's how it was until they started splitting them up into all them denumerations. But there's still only one religion— His up there." Michael the son-in-law chimes in: "And that's the one you belong to, Arch?"

Archie: "I'd be stupid not to, wouldn't I?"

So Archie is sure that all who do not agree with him are stupid.

When Archie talks to George Jefferson, the black comedian, he insists that God is white.

Archie: "God is the white man's God, ain't he?"

Jefferson: "What makes you think God isn't black?"

Archie: "Because God created man in his own image and you will note I ain't black."

Jefferson: "Well, don't complain to me about it."

Archie: "Look, you seen pictures of God, ain't you? That Dago artist painted him on that ceiling in Rome, remember?"

Jefferson: "You mean that white Dago painted him."

Archie: "Ever picture I ever seen of God he was white."

Jefferson: "You must have been looking at the negatives."

So Archie the God-maker makes God in his own image, projecting himself in every picture. And that is one of the reasons there is a bit of Archie Bunker in all of us. And it is only when the image of the false God fades that we see the image of the true God clearly.

WE MUST FACE OURSELVES

A distinguished clergyman once said, "I have had more trouble with myself than any other man I have ever met."

Probably all of us could say the same thing. Like the House of Mirrors at the carnival, no matter which way we turn we keep bumping into ourselves.

We marry amid the congratulations of our friends only to discover that the maintenance of a fine home is the problem of dealing with ourselves. We go into business with high hopes only to find that our major problem is ourselves.

When in the New Testament the Prodigal Son found himself at the bottom of the ladder in a hog pen, the record says "he came to himself." Shakespeare, the great dramatist, shifts the battlefields of the world to the problem of dealing with ourselves when he writes:

The fault, dear Brutus, is not in our stars,
But in ourselves, that we are underlings.

Despite the fact that dealing with ourselves is our major responsibility, we stubbornly refuse to recognize it. We either blame other people or the exterior circumstances under which we labor. We remember the words of Jesus who dealt with this problem: "Why do you look at the speck of sawdust in your brother's eye with never a thought for the plank in your own?"

No successful man has ever lived who has not dealt honestly with himself—his struggle with a terrible temper, a terrifying habit, a devastating disappointment. Failure to grapple with one's self will render us incapable of grappling with anyone else.

The heart of religion specifically deals with this matter; a man's relationship to his own soul, his invisible personality, the self-conscious being who thinks, purposes, loves. The basic question in life is, "What shall it profit a man if he shall gain the whole world and lose his soul?"

A poet, so the story goes, was ruined by a veiled figure who pursued him everywhere he went. He was in the act of making a fortune but the veiled figure snatched it from him. He was to be installed in the Hall of Fame but the veiled figure disgraced him.

On his wedding day the veiled figure stopped the mouth of the officiating priest by crying, "I forbid the banns."

"Who are you?" cried the poet, tearing away the veil. And lo, the face of the stranger was his own.

PULL YOURSELF TOGETHER

When I was a little fellow and my father caught me in some kind of foolish act he would say, "Pull yourself together." I find myself needing to do that today . . . pull myself together. Despite this overorganized age in which we live there is need for yet another "operation self-organization."

It is not easy to keep one's self "on the beam." Stephen Leacock said of one person "When he got on his horse he rode in all directions." H. G. Wells described one of his characters as "not so much a person as a civil war." Dwight L. Moody, once a popular evangelist, was asked what person gave him the most trouble in life. His reply was, "Myself."

How do we go about organizing ourselves? As the saying goes, how do we get it all together?

First, we must accept responsibility for ourselves. It was Will Rogers who said the three epochs in American history were (1) the passing of the Indian (2) the passing of the buffalo and (3) the passing of the buck. We are well in the third stage. We pass the buck. We blame our mistakes on something outside ourselves, heredity, environment . . . anything but ourselves. Adam started the buck passing business in the Garden of Eden. He said Eve gave him the apple. And we men have been nibbling on that apple core ever since. But if we are going to be honest with ourselves we must say what God said to David when he tried to evade responsibility: "Thou art the man."

Furthermore, in one's self-organization the matter of self-discipline is involved. Effective living means selective living. One cannot "cavort all over the lot" and expect to arrive at a place of consequence. If we do not discipline our lives there will soon be no life to discipline. We might well add another beatitude to Jesus' list: "Blessed are the disciplined for they shall inherit the earth."

Finally, self-organization means self-dedication. There is nothing that pulls a man together or keeps him together like his dedication to some worthy purpose in life. A group of high school students were on a field trip and made a casual visit to a local hospital. While they were there a boy who had been hit by a car was taken to the emergency ward with a broken leg. One of the visiting boys was asked to help carry the crippled boy to the operating room. It was a trip he never forgot. He became an orthopedic surgeon. Nothing so steadies a man as a steadfast look toward a worthy goal. It pulls him together.

JESUS HAD A SENSE OF HUMOR

Among the many art galleries of the world, have you ever seen a painting of Jesus with a smile on his face? It seems odd that the artists that painted Jesus have never assumed this thoroughly human carpenter of Nazareth had no sense of humor.

We have marvelous paintings of the Madonna and child . . . his beginning. We have magnificent paintings of the crucifixion and resurrection. But little in between. Why? Perhaps it is because we are so far removed from the sinless carpenter that we feel it a sacrilege to put him in the same category with us.

The evidences of Jesus' humor are abundant if we look for them. He said to his chief adversaries, the Pharisees, "You blind guides, you pay tithes of mint and dill and cummin, but you overlook weightier matters of justice, mercy and faith. You strain out a gnat and gulp down a camel." (Matt. 23:23)

They were observing the externals of the faith and ignoring the issues of the heart. Imagine them sipping tea in the courtyard when a gnat dives down in the cup. While they carefully squeeze out the gnat, a lumbering two humped camel worms his way into the Pharisee's mouth, hump after hump, until the last thing visible is the disappearing hind hoofs of the camel gently sliding down the esophagus of the dumbfounded Pharisee. I can imagine that laughter rocked the entire courtyard.

In another instance Jesus asked, "Can a blind man lead a blind man, lest both fall in a ditch? Why do you see the speck in your brother/s eye with never a thought for the log in your own?"

Here is irony that is unmistakably hilarious. In the sermon on the mount Jesus says, "Beware of false prophets who come to you in sheep's clothing but are ravenous wolves. Are grapes gathered from thorns or figs from thistles?" (Matt. 7:16)

Again, Jesus said, "It is easier for a camel to go through the eye of a needle than for a rich man to enter the kingdom of God." These little pen pictures in the mind, coupled with a fertile imagination, make for unforgettable truisms packed with real humor. Since he was a great teacher, he knew one picture would be worth more than a thousand words.

If we as individuals were asked what had helped us most to bear the burdens of life . . . religion or a sense of humor . . . it would be difficult to answer. We have been helped by both genuine religion and genuine humor.

In Jesus these two forces are conjoined. He was not only a man of sorrows and acquainted with grief; he was likewise a man of joy and acquainted with laughter.

ACT YOUR AGE

The biggest job any man is called upon to do is to grow up. The greatest tragedies I have ever seen are the people who become adults in body and remain as children in mind and spirit. Paul spoke to this point when he said, "When I was a child I spoke as a child . . . when I became a man I put away childish things."

Some people never grow up. Everybody loves a baby . . . unless the baby is sixty years old. It used to be that when our parents caught us in some childish trick they would say, "Act your age." This is not as easy as one would think.

We act our age when we are guided by truth instead of trivia. As adults we must learn the difference between fact and fancy. A child can live in a dream world and enjoy it; an adult must learn to see things as they really are. He must interpret the scene before him correctly lest his judgments be false.

We act our age when we meet crises with calmness instead of confusion. Blowing one's top over some trivial matter is to act like a child. I do not know it to be a fact but I have heard there is an inscription on a tombstone in France which reads; "Here lies Pierre Cabocard—a Baker, His grief-stricken widow dedicates this monument to his memory and reminds you she continues to serve delectable pastries at the same old shop—167 S. Rue St." A bit exaggerated, to be sure, but it shows how a mature person meets crisis calmly.

We act our age when we temper our strength with gentleness rather than hide our weaknesses with hostility. When we are touchy and oversensitive, when we bluster and shout, we are acting like children.

We act our age when our religious faith is purged of superstition and magic. There is a difference between believing in a loving God and believing in a cosmic magician. Paul said, "When I became a man I put away childish things." So must we.

WORDS ABOUT LOVE

Love is more than a characteristic of God: it is his character . . . Anonymous

Love is the key to the universe which unlocks all doors . . . Anonymous

Love is the only service that powers cannot command and money cannot buy . . . Anonymous

Love rules without a sword. Love binds without a cord . . . Anonymous

To love anyone is nothing else than to wish that person good . . . St. Thomas Aquinas

Of all earthly music, that which reaches farthest into heaven is the beating of a truly loving heart . . . Henry Ward Beecher

The true measure of loving God is to love him without measure . . . Bernard of Clairvaux

Any old woman can love God better than a doctor of theology can . . . St. Bonaventure

The mind has a thousand eyes, the heart but one; yet the light of a whole life dies, when love is done . . . Francis Bourdillon

Love is a tender plant; when properly nourished, it becomes

sturdy and enduring; but neglected, it withers and dies . . . Hugh Brown

Love isn't like a reservoir. You'll never drain it dry. It's much more like a natural spring. The longer and farther it flows, the stronger and the deeper and the clearer it becomes . . . Eddie Cantor

He prayeth best who loveth best, all things both great and small: For the dear God who loveth us, He made and loveth all . . . Samuel Taylor Coleridge

The pain of love be sweeter far than all other pleasures are . . . John Dryden

We are shaped and fashioned by what we love . . . Goethe

Love is the thing that enables a woman to sing while she mops up the floor after her husband has walked across it in his barn boots . . . Hoosier farmer

Where love is, there is God also . . . Leo Tolstoy

I know not where his islands lift their fronded palms in air: I only know I cannot drift beyond His love and care . . . John Greenlief Whittier

Better to have loved and lost, than not to have loved at all . . . Seneca

Love sought is good, but given unsought is better . . . Shakespeare

Not where I breathe, but where I love, I live . . . Robert Southwell

RESPECT YOURSELF

When we are reminded of the great commandment of Jesus, "Thou shalt love thy neighbor as thyself," the emphasis is usually placed on love of neighbor. But I want to shift the emphasis and talk a bit about the love of one's self. A person who does not have a high opinion of himself, you may be sure, will not have a high opinion of his neighbor.

What do we mean by self-respect? It certainly cannot be identified with egotism. The egoist, conceited and self-centered as he is, thinks too disparagingly of other people. An egotistical British professor once wrote by his name on the blackboard before his students, "Appointed personal physician to the king." A mischievous student scrawled underneath, "God save the king."

By self-respect we do not mean pride. Jesus denounced the pride of the Pharisees who gloated over the fact that they were "not as other people." It is impossible to lift ourselves by belittling others.

Self-respect is an awareness and appreciation of the high purposes to which man can give himself. It is involved in what Shakespeare had Polonius say to his nephew, Laertes, "This above all, to thine own self be true and it must follow as the night the day, thou canst not then be false to any man." Alfred Tennyson made reference to the sense of self-respect when he described Queen Victoria as being "loyal to the royal within herself."

The old Edinburgh weaver described self-respect beautifully when he prayed, "God help me to hold a high opinion of myself." A friend of mine was telling of the greatest temptation that ever came to him. He turned his back on it saying to himself: "No son of my father and mother would do a thing like that." He showed a high sense of self-respect.

Life is either desecration or consecration. The person who desecrates life makes of it a sacrilege; Nothing is sacred, neither himself, his neighbor nor God. Anything that desecrates human life is a sacrilege. Child labor is a sacrilege; the abusive use of drugs is a sacrilege; prostitution is a sacrilege; war is a sacrilege.

But life can be consecration—the commitment of oneself to the highest of human values, William Herbert Carruth says:

A picket frozen on duty,
A mother starved for her brood,
Socrates drinking the hemlock,
And Jesus on the rood;
And millions who, humble and nameless,
The straight, hard pathway plod—
Some call it Consecration,
And others call it God.

THE WORDS OF GOD

It may sound ridiculous, but I have the feeling that God has a problem of communication with his earthborn children. Adam and Eve either didn't get the message from God or they garbled it and lost the heritage of the garden of Eden.

Since God is alive and well, he is constantly speaking to us. What do you suppose some of the words are that he is using?

It could be that God's first word of communication is in his creation. If I wish to know what God is like, then I must examine his handiwork—the world he has made. It is God's laboratory, revealing the mysteries of life that has gone before us. Edna St. Vincent Millay expressed it beautifully when she wrote, "God, I can push the grass apart and lay my finger on Thy heart." God's record was written in the rocks millions of years ago. It suggests order, life reproducing its likeness, seeds invariably reproducing themselves. Creation seems to insist on cooperation.

At our fingertips are factors that sustain life and factors that destroy it. Hydrogen bombs wipe out cities and the inhabitants therein, but solar energy is inexhaustible and can be harnessed to preserve mankind.

God's second word to his children is in a book—the Bible. It is a record of the religious history of the Hebrew people in their relationship to the creator.

The Bible does not contain all the truth in the universe. Only God knows that. But God had to depend on men to write the Bible since God has no hands. These men of God talked about the Earth as having four corners (Rev. 20:8) since the people then thought the earth was flat. But the Bible does contain all the truth necessary for individual and world redemption.

The Ten Commandments are not true simply because they are in the Bible, but are true even if they had been left out of the scriptures. Stealing and lying and killing is simply contrary to the purposes of the creator.

I believe that God's third word is in a person—Jesus the carpenter. My eyes are human eyes and I can see only that which is human. I see truth best when it is incarnated in a truthful person. I see goodness best when incarnated in a good person. I see love best when incarnated in a lovely person.

All of my abstract ideas about God become concrete in the person of the carpenter of Nazareth. To be sure, there are millions of people who never heard of Jesus. Are they deliberately consigned to eternal perdition? Not if they see God as I see him in creation . . . in the Bible . . . and in a person.

ON BEING AWARE

Miriam Teichner once penned a poetic gem when she wrote: "God let me be aware. Let me not stumble blindly down the ways, just getting somehow safely through the days. Not even groping for another hand, not even wondering why it all was planned. Eyes to the ground, unseeking for the light. Soul never aching for a wild-winged flight. Please keep me eager just to do my share. God, let me be aware."

The art of awareness is the art of living up to one's maximum potential. It is awakening to the eternal miracle of life with its limitless possibilities. It is the art of keeping mentally alert, of being curious, observant and imaginative.

Awareness is striving to search the range of eye and ear, and taking time to look, listen and comprehend. It is the search for beauty in the flower, the butterfly, the bee, a dew drop, a sonnet, or a symphony. It is knowing wonder, awe and humility in the face of life's unexplained mysteries.

Awareness is the discovery of the mystic power of silence and listening to the secret voice of intuition. It is the identification of one's self with the hopes, dreams, fears and longings of other persons that we might the better understand them.

Awareness is enlarging the scope of one's life through the expansion of personality. Awareness is splitting the sky in two, and letting the face of God shine through.

Two thousand years ago a great teacher said: "Man shall not live by bread alone but by every word that proceeds from the mouth of God."

What are some of those words? They are words of beauty and harmony, truth and goodness, affection and friendship, aspiration and worship. God invites us to lift up our eyes to the splendor of the skies at midnight, to await the coming of the dawn from atop a mountain, to linger in the liveliness of the forest.

He has given us ears to listen to the sweet songs of the mockingbird, the rustling of the winds through the trees, the call of a coyote to its mate. Man lives not by bread alone but by the fragrance of roses, the scent of orange blossoms, the smell of mown hay, the clasp of a friend's hand, the tenderness of a mother's kiss.

Man lives not only by bread but by the lyrics of the poets, the wisdom of the sages, the holiness of the saints and the biographies of great souls.

One of our great philosphers, Immanuel Kant, said there were two things of which he was constantly aware: the starry heavens above and the moral law within.

THE MIRACLE OF ME

In this day of so many scientific and technological miracles it is easy to overlook the fact that man himself is the greatest of them all. The vastness of the known universe is staggering. What is more staggering is the mind of man who can survey it. Greater than the stars are the astronomers who can measure their distances and estimate their ages.

I once heard of a minister whose sermon title was "The Miracle of Me." I do not know what he said but I do know the human body is the miracle of God's creativity. The body is a veritable chemical plant more complex than any man has ever built. Food taken in the body is transformed into skin, muscle, blood, bones, teeth, even heat and movement. Despite vigorous activity the body maintains a uniform temperature, releasing heat energy when it is cold and a cooling system by evaporation from the skin when it is warm.

The human hand is a marvel of mechanical adaptability. What other mechanical device can thread a needle or perform a delicate heart operation?

The human eye is one of the most delicate and, certainly, one of the most useful instruments of the body. Since too much light can injure the eye there is an automatic diaphragm called the pupil which automatically adjusts to various levels of light. No camera manufacturer has ever been able to perfect an instrument as sensitive in automatic focusing as the human eye.

The ear is as amazing as the eye. The outer ear collects sound waves and reflects them to the eardrum. The extremely sensitive nerve fibers in the cochlea can distinguish some fifteen hundred tones in a span of ten octaves. Furthermore, the ear is self-adjusting so that it can hear the roar of a cannon or the footfall of a cat without injury.

The heart is perhaps the most important and certainly the most amazing organ of the body. During the average lifetime it pumps enough blood to fill a string of tank cars fifty miles long, without a single shutdown for repairs. The only rest it gets is the fleeting pause between beats.

I cannot believe that this miraculous man accidentally sprang from primordial ooze. It seems more reasonable to believe that the writer of the book of Genesis had it right when he said, "In the beginning, God created . . . man" . . . In His own miraculous image.

THE CAT THAT COULD NOT BACK DOWN

Sometime ago I saw a newspaper account of a cat that had climbed a tree and had gotten so far out on the small branches that it could not back down. It cried piteously all night and the local fire department finally had to come to the rescue.

I have known people who could have saved themselves many unhappy experiences if they had learned the gentle art of backing down at the proper time. Because of pride, stubbornness, fear or conceit, they refuse to admit their mistakes, refuse to back down.

Damascus blades are made of the finest steel and will bend double under pressure. But when the pressure is released they spring back into perfect shape again. Cast iron, however, the lowest grade of metal, will break before it will bend a mere fraction. An unbending, unrelenting will is a low grade piece of character; a reasonable, yielding person shows evidence of finer spiritual achievement.

If a person is unwilling to admit his mistakes he is often forced to defend every foolish statement, keep every rash promise, make good on every threat. I know two young business associates who were involved in a heated argument over policy. When neither would back down, the partnership was dissolved and the families have been feuding every since.

I know of more than one church that has been rendered powerless because of ancient feuds. When neither side in the argument has the Christian grace to say, "We are sorry," the church is doomed to extinction.

I have known dozens of young couples who have allowed some petty quarrel to drive a wedge between them, wreck their homes and destroy their marriage. He who refuses to back down at the proper time makes an unreasonable business partner, an irritating traveling companion, a tyrannical boss, an unlovable parent and an impossible marital partner.

I would like to add one additional Beatitude to those mentioned in the Bible: "Blessed are they who have the Christian grace to say "I'm sorry." These two words, sincerely spoken, can save us from a lot of trouble.

ON THAT FIRST EASTER SUNDAY

In a London park, there is an obelisk monument erected in memory of Edith Cavell. During the First World War (1914–18), Miss Cavell, daughter of a British clergyman, ran an escape route for Belgian soldiers fleeing from the overpowering German army, which was plundering their country. German authorities tried her, convicted her and executed her before a firing squad. The monument erected in her memory had only one word carved in granite—"Dawn." That one word reminds us of Easter Sunday morning.

Easter marks the dawn of the mighty idea of the incarnation of God in human flesh. Evidently God has a problem of communication with his children. So he sent his son Jesus to make visible God's will to men.

All of God that could be contained in one human being was incarnated in Jesus. We Christians do not equate God the creator with Jesus the revealer. But we insist that Jesus is the human (knowable) side of God.

When Jesus talked about our relationship with other people, "love thy neighbor," "turn the other cheek," we feel it is God speaking to us.

Easter marks the dawn of the idea of the eternal presence of God among men. We worship at no sealed tomb. The stone has been rolled away and the tomb is empty. The spirit of God through Christ has been let loose in the world. Tombs can no more contain the resurrected Christ than a box can contain the light from the sun. Christ is alive and well. He has broken the shackles of death for all who proclaim him Lord. Easter marks the dawn of the idea of the ultimate triumph of God. Evil men may crucify his son and put him in a sealed tomb. But they cannot keep him there.

On the first Easter Sunday morning the disciples saw him through the reality of a spiritual experience. Their eyes did not deceive them. Nor did they invent the story. Would anyone invent such a story only to be crucified head down, as was Peter? Or to get his head chopped off such as Paul? Or to be stoned to death such as Stephen?

This spiritual experience can be the experience of anyone who wishes to see him. He is only a prayer away.

THE MIRACLE OF LOVE

Love in a person's life makes all the difference in the world, the difference between sainthood and satan. Victor Hugo wrote: "Life is the flower of which love is the honey."

Where there is genuine love there is God. A Protestant minister in France once rescued a Jewish peddler from a mob threatening to do him harm. He brought him into his home and asked him to eat dinner with his family. By coincidence the Catholic priest dropped by for a chat.

The mood of the evening was mellow as the priest turned to the minister and said, "I surely wish you and I were of the same religion." The minister put one arm around the priest and the other around the Jew and said, "Those who love God are of the same religion."

Though every person should have a high opinion of himself, self-love is self-destructive. In the town of Leamington, England, there is an inscription on a tombstone that I shall never forget:
Here lies a miser who lived for himself,
And cared for nothing but gathering pelf.
Now where he is or how he fares,
Nobody knows and nobody cares.

What a contrast is the inscription at St. Paul's Cathedral, London:
Sacred to the memory of General George Gordon, who at all times and everywhere gave his strength to the weak, his sustenance to the poor, his sympathy to the suffering and his heart to God.

Love expresses itself most beautifully when it reaches out to the unlovely. Some years ago I visited the home of a family of a darling three-year-old girl. "Do you want to see my dollies?" she asked. Telling her I could hardly wait, she brought out one by one an entire family of dolls. "What is your favorite?" I asked.

She hesitated for a moment, then asked me to wait until she could bring out her favorite. It was a dilapidated old doll with no hair, a broken nose, one arm and one leg. "Why do you like this one the best?" I asked.

"I love her most," she said, "because if I didn't love her, no one else would."

YOU HAVE ONE GOOD EYE

A local woman recently told me a story that I want to share with you. While she was busy about the morning chores the door bell rang, when she went to the door, accompanied by her four-year-old daughter, she saw an elderly man who wanted to sell her a broom.

His clothes were dirty, his whiskers were untrimmed, his hands were filthy, his old hat was slouchy and he had a black patch over his right eye. While the mother was purchasing the broom to encourage the old man, the daughter was looking the visitor over from head to toe.

As the vendor delivered the broom and started to leave, the little girl, never at a loss for words, said "Mister, you sure do have one good eye."

When I heard this story I could not help but think of the tremendous importance it is for all of us to catch something of the philosophy of that little girl.

Having been trained by her mother to be tidy in her dress, she could not compliment him on his rumpled clothes, his unkempt whiskers, his dirty hands. But she searched long enough to find the one thing for which she could praise him and, in her uninhibited way, she blurted out, "Mister, you sure do have one good eye."

Finding fault is a favorite indoor sport for many people. We can spend hours faulting government officials in Washington, Austin and City Hall. If we have no breath left we can chew out the neighbors next door or the clerk at the supermarket. But I can imagine that, together, we could make for ourselves a better neighborhood and a better nation if we would make a habit of finding something complimentary to say about every person we meet.

If nothing good could be said, we could at least withhold judgment a little longer. It is said that when Darrell Royal came to coach the Texas Longhorns some years ago, one of the most influential persons among the alumni called him and said, "Coach, some of my friends and I want to take you to lunch and give you some constructive criticism; do you want to hear it?"

Coach Royal said, "No, I don't." The man persisted, "You mean you don't want constructive criticism?"

"No," said Royal, "I don't want criticism of any kind. I work better under friendship, support and compliments."

Don't you suppose we all work better when complimented rather than when criticized? I think there is something sublime in this quatrain:

There is so much good in the worst of us,
And so much bad in the best of us,
That it hardly behooves any of us,
To talk about the rest of us.

A WINDOW OVER THE SINK

Years ago, so the story goes, a fire practically destroyed the farm home of an elderly couple in the White Mountains of New Hampshire. The beloved couple, in their sixties, were left not only homeless but broken-hearted. All that they had accumulated in a lifetime of hard work had been destroyed—the bronzed shoes of the babies, pictures of the children growing up, everything.

Because they were so well liked by the community the local minister determined to raise enough money to replace the home. There was such a fine response on the part of the neighbors that there was not only enough money to rebuild the house, but there would be a few dollars left over. So the minister asked the woman, "What would you like for us to put into this new house that you did not have in the old one, something you really wanted but felt you never could afford?"

Possibly the woman's mind had been made up before the question was asked. She said, "For the last forty years I have stood over the kitchen sink washing dishes and have had to look at a blank wall. Just beyond that wall are the beautiful White Mountains. I wish you would put a window over the sink so I could see the mountains."

And for the rest of her life some of the drudgery of dishwashing was removed because this woman could see the beautiful mountains in the distance. The view lifted her above the petty and irritating annoyances of the daily routine of life. It reminds us of the words of the Psalmist, "I will lift up mine eyes unto the hills. From whence cometh my help? My help cometh from the Lord."

Too often we find ourselves as the woman at the kitchen sink. Confined by the walls of our own prejudices we impoverish ourselves when we limit our friendships only to those of our own kind. No true believer in American democracy has a right to isolate himself from other people in the family of mankind. We all need windows to look out upon the world about us.

Quite often we confine ourselves behind the walls of our own ignorance. From my study window I can see scores of university students rushing in and out of the library doors. Unsatisfied with the limitations of their present understanding they look out the windows to the great mountain peaks of truth bequeathed to them by their forebears.

It is to the credit of the people in the United States that on any given Sunday morning some forty million of them find their way to a place of worship because their spirits hunger for more than the mundane world can give them. They are looking through the window over the sink to the mountains from whence cometh their help.

THE LEGEND OF THE SKYLARK

One of the most beautiful poems ever written was that of the nineteenth-century poet, Percy B. Shelley, entitled "Ode to a Skylark." He describes this bird as one, though very ordinary looking, but with a song that is hauntingly beautiful.

It gets its name from the fact that it flies higher in the sky than any other bird its size, usually in the early evening during the setting of the sun. As it gently coasts earthward, one can hear the graceful lilting notes of the skylark from hundreds of yards in the air.

There is a legend to the effect that as a skylark once started its high climb toward the stars, it noticed a curious little man pushing a cart and singing a song. "What are you singing about?" asked the skylark. "About my worms" said the little man, "I have the finest worms for sale that can be found anywhere."

"Worms, eh?" as the skylark came closer. "What do you ask for them?" "One feather per worm," said the little man.

The skylark looked at the delicious worms. Then it looked at its wings. There were hundreds of feathers on them. What difference would it make if he exchanged just one feather for a nice, juicy worm? So he traded one feather for a worm.

Darting upward toward the sky, it discovered it could fly as high and sing as beautiful as before. This pleasing experience became the story of the skylark's life. Each evening it plucked out a feather in exchange for a worm. As the skylark became heavier, its wings became thinner. One day it was distressed to find that it could neither fly quite so high nor sing so well. Finally it could neither fly nor sing.

The skylark busied itself digging in the dirt and found a sizable pile of worms. When the little man with his cart came by, the skylark said, "Little man, I want my feathers back. Here are worms enough and to spare." But the little man shouted over his shoulder, "Worms for feathers is my business . . . not feathers for worms." And that is the end of the story. Or is it?

Hosts of people have sacrificed their dreams and hopes for the future, for the tempting morsel of the present. Don't compromise yourself in the ways of the wicked. Don't surrender that first feather.

ON BEING MISERABLE

Here is a prescription for being miserable in case you are interested. Most any doctor will guarantee results if you mix the following ingredients together.

First: Feel sorry for yourself. Compare your lot in life to all the people around you who have more money, better jobs, better homes and easier lifestyles than you. Engage in self-pity and insist that your troubles are the result of bad breaks or that God has singled you out as a born loser.

Second: Cultivate the habit of being a worry wart. Particularly, you should worry over the things that have already happened. If I had married Jean instead of Jane or Jim instead of John, what a whale of a difference it would have made. Worry over things that are inevitable, such as old age or death. Worry over things that never happen. In case you go to a ball game, don't forget that the stadium could fall down; in case of a plane flight, dwell on the thought that planes do collide in the air.

Third: Complain and share your complaints and gripes with all who will listen. Count that day lost if you have not vented your wrath upon the government, City Hall, the school system, the children in the neighborhood, the barking dogs at night.

Fourth: Have it your way. What does it matter when you lose a friend if you win the argument? The way you look at the situation is the only sensible way. Don't let people push you around. When the chips are down, take good care of yourself.

Fifth: Be sarcastic. Ridicule some unfortunate dirty beggar if you can get a laugh out of it. He could do better if he wanted to work.

Sixth: Ignore spiritual resources. Religion is a crutch for people who will not take care of themselves. Prayer is usually talking to yourself. The Bible is a collection of old wives' tales and miracles that never happened. If there is a God, he neither knows nor cares if we exist.

You don't have to break a leg to be miserable. Just follow these rules to the letter and if you're not miserable within a week . . . you are not normal.

GETTING ALONG WITH OTHERS

Benjamin Franklin was a wise old diplomat in the early days of American history. He had much to do with making the United States a nation to be reckoned with after it gained its independence.

He had the unusual ability to get other persons to follow his leadership. In his own words, he tells us the secret of his success: "I will speak ill of no man; I will speak of all of the good I know of everybody."

It takes some of us a long time to learn that we do not win friends and influence people by argumentative methods. When we deal with people we are not dealing with creatures of logic but creatures of emotion, bristling with prejudice, largely motivated by pride. When we think we win an argument, we usually lose a friend. If you crush a man's pride, you generally make another enemy.

Andrew Carnegie paid Charles Schwab the unprecedented salary of a million dollars a year to run U.S. Steel. It was not that Schwab knew more about steel than Carnegie, but because Schwab could get better work out of more people than anyone else.

Here was his secret: "I consider my ability to arouse enthusiasm among men the greatest asset that I possess. The way to get a man to do his best is to show him your appreciation. I am always anxious to praise and loath to find fault."

Are you having a little argument with your husband or wife? Are you finding that growing children have a mind of their own and do not respond to your stern commands? Try something different. Look for something positively good to say . . . and say it often.

Some years ago our son brought back his first report card from college. He received four A's and one C. My first question was, "What is the reason for this C?" I didn't say, "I'm so proud of you for the four A's." I know better now.

Philosopher John Dewey said man's deepest urge is the desire to be important. If this is true, think of the opportunity we have to give the people we meet each day some well deserved appreciation. I'm not talking about flattery which is only from the teeth out, but honest appreciation is from the heart.

LINCOLN'S WORDS ARE NOT ATHEISTIC

For more than a century his bitterest opponents have said that Abraham Lincoln was an infidel who frequently quoted the Bible and used religious terminology for political purposes. One of his chief critics was William Herndon, Lincoln's former law partner in Springfield, Illinois.

Undoubtedly Herndon was prejudiced against the president because Lincoln knew Herndon to be heavily addicted to the use of alcohol. Consequently the president refused to give Herndon the political appointment of public trust which he sought.

His biographers seem to agree that there were two Lincolns; the Lincoln of pre-White House days and the President Lincoln of the United States. In his earlier life, Lincoln was a victim of doubts, personal, political and religious. But the mature Lincoln who became president was, we believe, a deeply religious man.

Lincoln had a devotedly religious mother, and never seemed to get far away from the early religious truths he learned at her knee. While he did falter at times between faith and doubt, confidence and despair, this has been the experience of millions of sincere Christians. Changing question marks into exclamation points is part of the process of religious growth.

Let us review the words of Lincoln when he left Springfield for Washington:

"I leave now, not knowing when, or whether ever I shall return, with a task before me greater than that which rested on the shoulders of Washington. Without the assistance of the Divine Being, who always attended him, I cannot succeed. With that assistance I cannot fail.

"Trusting in Him who can go with me and remain with you and be everywhere for good, let us confidently hope that all will be well."

Does this sound like an atheist speaking?

Lincoln wrestled for a long time over the Emancipation Proclamation. Before signing it he said, "I know there is a God and that He hates prejudice and slavery. I see the storm coming and I know He has a hand in it. If He has a work for me I believe I am ready. I am nothing; but truth is everything. I know I am right for Christ teaches it."

President Lincoln was usually present in pew No. 14 in the New York Avenue Presbyterian Church where Dr. James Gurley was minister. Dr. Gurley said the president probably would have joined the church had not the assassin's bullet cut short his life. Surely the spirit of the living Christ lived in his heart, even as his memory lives today in the hearts of his countrymen.

YET

In Detroit near Grand Avenue and Woodward Boulevard is Metropolitan Church. On the church lawn is the statue of a young man with a serpent coiling its body around his legs. It is the work of Gutzon Borglum. The sculptor once dropped in to a worship service here when the minister was preaching from the Seventy-first Psalm: "I will yet praise Him." In the course of the sermon the minister told about how the Psalmist and the Hebrew people had come upon great difficulty, their little country having been invaded by ruthless conquerors from all directions, their people having been pillaged and finally taken into Babylonian captivity. But the Psalmist's faith was indestructible. In spite of all, he said "I will yet praise Him."

Mr. Borglum was so impressed with the service that he carved the statue of the young man being encircled by the serpent as a remembrance. Underneath the statue is one word: "Yet"

I like that word. It is bulging with muscle, power, courage, strength. It reminds me of Helen Keller . . . as a child blind, deaf, dumb. But she went from there to graduate with honors from a university, write several significant books, lecture throughout the world and raise millions of dollars for the education of the blind. I only heard her speak one time. Her concluding sentence was, "I am grateful to God for my blessings." "I will yet praise Him."

That word "yet" reminds me of Dr. Tom Dooley standing knee deep in bandages in Laos treating the poor, the diseased and the crippled people of that impoverished country. The doctors told him he should look after his own cancer-ravaged body but he stayed in his post of duty until he couldn't stand any longer. He was entirely too young to die but no word of complaint escaped his lips. Rather he thanked God daily for his blessings. "I will yet praise Him."

Just last week I read of a girl who three years ago had been robbed, raped, shot and left by the roadside to die. Her entire left side was paralyzed . . . but she lived. She cannot speak, her vocal cords were destroyed. But last month she received her high school diploma . . . with high honors. She plans to spend the rest of her life in inspiring other people to overcome their handicaps. She already has! "I will yet praise Him."

CONTINUING PROBLEMS

"It is a gloomy moment in the history of our country. Not in the lifetime of most men has there been so much grave and deep apprehension. Never has the future seemed so incalculable as at this time. The domestic economic situation is in chaos. Our dollar is weak throughout the world. Prices are so high as to be utterly impossible. The political cauldron seethes and bubbles with uncertainty. Russia hangs as usual like a cloud, dark and silent upon the horizon. It is a solemn moment in history. Of our troubles no man can see the end."

When do you suppose the above paragraph was written? Certainly not last week—not even in your lifetime. It was written 123 years ago, in Harpers Magazine in 1857.

It demonstrates that we have always had world-shaking problems to face—and probably always will.

The present world obviously is a powder keg and a lot of people are playing with matches. One atomic bomb on Washington or Moscow could start international war.

It is estimated that in the year A.D. 2,000 there will be 6.5 billion people in the world, and 33 percent of them will be slowly starving to death.

What shall we do? Throw up our hands? Give up hope for tomorrow? Never. That is a coward's way out.

It seems to me that the harder we fall after a calamity, the higher we bounce back. Let me illustrate.

In the early part of the twentiety century boll weevils almost wiped out the cotton crops of the southeastern United States. What did the farmers do? They planted peanuts and made more money with less work.

On the public square in Enterprise, Alabama, there is a monument to the boll weevil. The inscription reads: "In profound appreciation of the boll weevil that brought us prosperity."

Hanging in the Tate Gallery of London is Watt's great painting called *Hope*. A dejected woman is sitting on the world, playing a harp with only one string. That is the artist's picture of hope, triumphant over everything hurtful to mankind.

Dare we give up hope for tomorrow? Not if we keep cool heads and warm hearts and follow the leadership of our creator.

MODERN MIRACLES

Several years ago I spent a few days in a village at the foot of Mount Blanc in the French Alps. It is called Mount Blanc because its lofty summit is crowned with snow throughout the year.

While feasting my eyes on the beauty surrounding me, I saw God pass a miracle directly in front of me. Through a rift in the clouds above me I saw a shaft of sunlight on a stagnant pool of water near a riding stable. The water was obviously filthy, but the rays of the sun seemed to be lifting it toward the sky to form more clouds.

These new clouds were driven by the wind to hover atop Mount Blanc and shroud it in momentary darkness. When the clouds drifted away I could see in my imagination a new mantle of snow glistening in the sunlight and crowning the gigantic peak. Here was a modern miracle that God had performed before my eyes. The stagnant, dirty germ-filled water had been lifted from the earth, suspended in the air, transformed into beautiful snowflakes and transported to the mountain top.

It takes the resources of God and the entire universe to make beautiful snowflakes out of stagnant water. The human body also is a miracle. How two microscopic human cells can unite to form this complex machine called the human body is more than we can understand.

To be sure, scientists can tell us everything that happens from conception to the grave but the matter of why certain things happen as they do, is beyond comprehension. To assume that we can put God out of business by mastering the laws of creation is to assume the ridiculous.

The more we know the more we realize we don't know. It is probably true that the greatest miracles are neither in the realm of nature nor in human nature. They are in the realm of the spirit.

For instance, I knew a person who, two years ago, confessed that he had committed every sin known to the human race. But something, evidently tremendously important, happened to him. That something changed his thought patterns, his actions, his habits, his character.

If God can transform germ-filled drops of water into pure snow-flakes, if He can transform the wayside puddle, through the moon-light, into a silver mirror, surely He can redeem the lives of his children. If we have the eyes to see, it is happening all about us. The key word is commitment.

WORKAHOLICS

In the United States, work is a four-letter word that is lauded, praised, expected and usually demanded. Most of us delight in telling our friends how early we go to work and how late we labor.

We have the feeling that the more work we do the more success we will have. We work on extra jobs for extra money to buy the things we don't need to impress the people we don't even like.

There was a time when working twelve or fifteen hours a day was called economic slavery. Nowadays it is called moonlighting.

This is not to say that a workaholic is a menace. We are all eternally grateful for work. Without it we would go crazy. But the fact remains that all work and no play makes Jack a dull boy. We parents often teach our children that they justify their existence by the work they do. Here is a quote from an Associated Press story:

"Amy, fifteen, had always gotten straight A's in school and her parents were extremely upset when she got a B on her report card. 'If I fail in what I do,' Amy told her parents, 'I fail in what I am.'" This message was part of Amy's suicide note.

We are stunned when statisticians tell us that suicides among teenagers have almost doubled within the last two decades and that half of those in our nation's psychiatric wards are under twenty-one years of age. There are many reasons for this phenomenon but the bottom line could be the belief that the sole means of success is measured by the high marks received.

There are things worse than living without hard work. One of them is to work without living. Samuel Johnson said it best: "No man is obliged to work every waking hour; he must have a part of his life to himself."

To work too hard and too long is to take work too seriously. Workaholics need to develop the capacity to engage in creative recreation. Getting one's self untangled from having his eye on the ball, his ear to the ground and his shoulder to the wheel could be the means of a longer and a happier life.

God, who enjoined us to labor, likewise enjoined us to rest. Both are essential for abundant living.

THE MANUSCRIPTS OF GOD

God's manuscripts are the truths he writes with his own hand on the universe in which he has placed us. His most profound truth is recorded in the first five words of the Bible: "In the beginning, God created . . ." The trouble is that so many of us accept the gift with little regard for the giver. We carelessly take for granted the provisions God has made for our existence without so much as a courteous thanks.

Since God is a dependable God, ours is a dependable universe. We are not here simply by chance but by choice. For instance, the earth rotates on its axis at the rate of a thousand miles an hour. If it rotated at the rate of a hundred miles an hour, our days and nights would be 10 times as long as they are now. So our days would be too hot for any type of life by day and too cold for life by night.

Again, the sun, source of all life, has a surface temperature of some 12,000 degrees Fahrenheit and the earth is conveniently some ninety-three million miles away, making life on earth liveable. If the sun's temperature were 1,200 degrees or 100,000 degrees, our planet would be a frigid iceberg or a burning cinder.

Furthermore, if the moon, which is some 240,000 miles away, were only 50,000 miles from the earth, our ocean tides would be so enormous that the water would cover our tallest mountains twice each day. This would mean the destruction of all life on land, even the mountains themselves.

A most startling fact is that if there were no oxygen in the atmosphere there would be no animate life either on land or sea. But if the atmosphere contained 50 percent oxygen instead of the present 21 percent, all combustible objects would either burn or explode.

It is obvious to me that the facts concerning the world in which we live cannot be reconciled with the laws of chance. The writer of the book of Genesis gave utterance to a profound truth, "In the beginning God created . . ." Ours is not a mindless universe going blind. If we see design in the world about us, surely there must be a designer. If we see plan in an acorn which ultimately becomes an oak tree, surely there must be a planner. If we see order in the moving of the stars above us, surely there must be one who orders. There are none so blind as those who, having eyes, refuse to see the manuscripts of truth which God has written with his own hand.

IS GOD ON OUR SIDE?

Theologians through the centuries have told us that human beings are made in the image or likeness of God. We are endowed with the power, under God, to determine our own future and the power to choose our own destinies.

This distinguishes the sons and daughters of Adam and Eve from all the other creatures that God has created. We were made in his image.

It seems, however, that mortals have a tendency to turn this phrase "made in God's image" completely around. We want to make God into our image. For instance, there are whites so prejudiced against blacks that they actually believe God put a curse on them to make them black.

Is the God we worship one who handicaps two-thirds of his children by making their skin darker than our own? Are we stupid enough to insist that color is more important than character? I can't believe it. It is impossible to saddle our prejudices on God.

We know the Bible to be a series of sixty-six books written by the prophets of God over a period of about fourteen hundred years between 1200 B.C. and A.D. 200. Literally hundreds of the saints of the ages made their contribution to this Holy Book— the book about God.

From the ancient concept of God who walked in the garden of Eden in the cool of the day, lived atop Mt. Sinai and was the tribal God of Israel alone, to the universal God of the vast expanse of creation we know today, there is a progressive revelation of truth that staggers human imagination.

Nevertheless, there are those who will insist that God is particularly partial to the United States simply because they are U.S. citizens. And if an earthquake completely swallowed the citizens of Russia, there would be millions of people here who would say God did it. They seek to bend God into their own image.

The God I see in Christ on the cross praying for those who were killing him, is not a God who goes about killing people. The God of the Universe cannot possibly be made into our likeness and still be God.

KNEEL AT HIS FEET

Several years ago, while in Copenhagen, Denmark, a group of us visited the downtown cathedral to view the work of the internationally famous sculptor, Bertel Thorvaldssen.

Our guide showed us the statues of the first six apostles on the south side of the cathedral and the remainder of the apostles on the north side. The sculptor had the ability to translate into marble something of the character of each of the apostles as depicted within the pages of the New Testament.

Then our guide took us to the high altar of the church. "Here," he said, "we see the masterpiece of the sculptor as he depicted the Christ in marble.

"But," he said with genuine reverence "before you can see his face, you must kneel at his feet." Instinctively we all knelt at the altar, and as we lifted our eyes from the kneeling position we could see that underneath the roof beams was a shaft of light coming directly from the face of Christ.

Since then, I have pondered upon this unforgettable picture—we see Christ best from a kneeling position. It may be that for days on end we do not even give God a second thought; then tragedy strikes, and we are thrown to our knees. Only then do we pray.

Real prayer is not an endeavor to alter the purposes of God but to alter ourselves that the will of God may be done through us. When we earnestly pray, we link ourselves with the inexhaustible power that spins the universe. Through the eyes of Christ we see God as Father, yearning for the return of his wayward son, seeking with the shepherd the one lost sheep out of a hundred in the fold.

Prayer is Abraham Lincoln saying "I have been driven many times to my knees in the overwhelming conviction that there is nowhere else to go." Prayer is the practice of the presence of God. Prayer is the courage to pray "Thy will be done in me."

ON BEING HELPFUL

The older I get, the less I like to be waited on and the more I like to be helpful to others. I have read the book *Looking Out For Number One* and I am willing to admit I wouldn't enjoy doing so if I could.

When I am busy in the service of others, I do not look upon myself as conferring favors, but paying my debts. I must spend the rest of my life in helping others in order to give in the same measure I have received from others.

We salute the thousands of helpful citizens who are just now walking the streets and going from house to house to ensure the success of the United Way Campaigns throughout America. Every institution served by the United Way is a service institution which makes for better and healthier citizens in a more wholesome neighborhood. It is a way of saying that we care for all of our neighbors and want to extend a helping hand wherever and whenever it is needed.

I have a personal reason for being grateful for the dedicated services of scouting movement in our community. The Cubmaster and Scoutmaster in America is engaged in one of the most exciting tasks known, that of working with youth.

He leads young persons by arousing their enthusiasm, charging them with ideals, guiding them in these perilous times with his presence and his stability. His only pay is the deep personal satisfaction of knowing that he has contributed immeasurably to the development of the kind of citizen America needs.

When we think of the people who are helpful to us, we must not forget the woman in the kitchen who prepares the family meals, often without praise. I don't know who wrote it but it was a prayer of a housewife which went as follows:

"Lord of all pots and pans and tins, since I've not time to be a saint by doing lovely things, or watching late with thee, or dreaming in the twilight, or storming heaven's gates, make me a saint by getting meals and washing up the plates.

"Warm all the kitchen with thy love and light it with thy peace; forgive me all my worrying and make all my grumbling cease. Thou who did love to give men food—in room or by the sea—Accept this service that I do, I do it unto thee."

The best portion of a good man's life is the unremembered acts of kindness and love. No man is useless in the world who lightens the burden of another.

ON GETTING OFF THE EARTH

I am not impressed when fictional scientists announce that, in the world of tomorrow, people will be able to take scheduled trips to the moon or some other journey in interstellar space. But I do think that much of the pleasure of staying on the earth comes from knowing how to get off. This can be done without spaceships or mirrors. Here are some of the ways to do it.

A good book gives wings to the mind, enables a man to soar to worlds unknown.

There is no frigate like a book
To take us miles away.

A man is poor indeed who has not known the joy of being lifted out of himself by a great book. Through a good book a man can visit the king's palace in Babylon, fantastic Egypt under the pharaohs, the ancient temples of the Greeks, the daily life of the aborigines in Australia. No man need be bored as long as he can enjoy the companionship of great books.

Love has the power to send a man whirling into the atmosphere. The saddest people I know are those who are all wrapped up in a little package called "self" and who either do not have or do not cultivate the capacity to concern themselves with other people. Silas Marner was a miserable old miser who hated the world and everyone in it until Eppie, the homeless little girl, came into his life. Love is the spark of life that lifts us to greatness. Without love there would be neither great literature, great music, or great art. Love is the essence of God himself.

Prayer is man's best method of getting out of this world. The magic carpet of Baghdad was only an instrument of magic in a fairy world. But prayer, personal communion with God, enables us to move into the higher atmosphere of the spiritual. Through prayer we get a God's-eye view of the world. Prayer releases the mighty energies of the human soul. Prayer is a person's most effective road to peace, most effective vision of God. Edna St. Vincent Millay said it like this:

The soul can split the sky in two
And let the face of God shine through.

AVOID CYNICISM LIKE PLAGUE

In one of the newer translations of the New Testament, the word "sneer" is used several times. "The Pharisees who were fond of money . . . sneered at him" [Jesus]. "At the crucifixion, the people stood and looked on and sneered."

"On the day of Pentecost when the power of God moved in the lives of men, some of the people sneered."

That is the mood of a great number of people in our day. Three sneers for everything. Three cheers for nothing. The cult of the scornful is growing in numbers. The mood of the cynic is in danger of engulfing us.

The great enemy of Christianity is not intellectual skepticism but moral cynicism. Our trouble is not that the majority of our people disagree with the basic beliefs of the Christian faith. It is that they are cynical about the entire process of life . . . its values, its possibilities, its goals, its ultimate purposes.

The first step of the cynic is loss of faith in people in general. David in his haste said that all men are liars, and the cynic, after mature deliberation is saying the same thing today. Thomas Carlyle, the Scotch cynic of the eighteenth century, insisted that democracy was absurd, that the rights of the majority should be denied, that dictatorship was superior to democracy and that the majority opinion could not be trusted.

It seems that the despair of the eighteenth century is returning to haunt us in the twentieth. Obviously, it is not easy to keep one's faith in human possibilities. A good part of this century has been spent in the pursuit of war and the atrocities of the enemies. Hitler's gas chambers, Japanese death marches and the slaughter of innocent women and children in Vietnam are still vivid in our memories.

But we dare not lose faith in the future. God does not damn us with continuing wars. We damn ourselves. We can have a world of relative peace and prosperity if we, the nations of the earth are willing to pay the price of obtaining it.

The second step of the cynic is the loss of faith in himself. If he says that all men are liars he will soon become a liar himself. If he says that all men are cheats and frauds he himself will become a cheat and a fraud. If he says the future of mankind is hopeless, he will soon realize that his own future is hopeless. Sooner or later, man actually becomes what he thinks.

The final step of the cynic is loss of faith in God. Thomas Carlyle once stood on a bridge overlooking the slum areas of the city of Glasgow and said with acid bitterness: "Think of it, amid all of this human misery before us, God does nothing about it." Many of us are like Carlyle, putting the blame on God instead of ourselves.

SYMBOL OF DESTRUCTION
BECOMES SHRINE OF LOVE

Some years ago I had the good fortune to spend a day in Coventry, England. I remembered the days during the war when German planes under Adolph Hitler had pummeled the daylights out of the area and had mercilessly destroyed the magnificent cathedral at the heart of the city. Both the city and cathedral have long since been rebuilt and Coventry today is one of the most beautiful cities in England.

In the heart of the city is a mall where the people can leisurely walk amidst the charming environment of green grasses, flowers and fountains without having to dodge the constant flow of traffic. The lovely cathedral is located in the center of the mall.

The forecourt of the cathedral is built on the nave of the Old Cathedral and one can see in the courtyard the broken traceries of the charred walls of past years. Where the high altar of the old Cathedral once stood, there is a pile of rocks crowned by a cross made from charred wood salvaged from the old roof. Behind the cross are these words: "Father, forgive!"

In order to put action behind those words of love, a group of German Christians gave a year of their lives in hard labor during the rebuilding of the cathedral.

What was once a symbol of hate and destruction has now become a sign of love and forgiveness for the entire world to see. Two thousand years ago the man from Nazareth endured the agony of the cross because his enemies exercised the human power at their disposal to destroy him. But in the last breath of his life he appropriated divine power and said: "Father, forgive them; for they know not what they do."

This kind of love for one's enemies is rarely seen today. But the test of one's faith in the way of the man from Nazareth is determined, not by the number of times he prays, but by his willingness to get off his knees, seek out the person he likes least and say, "I'm sorry."

If that person is not readily available, there is a telephone around, or a stamp to carry a letter. Forgiving love could make for happier days . . . and longer life. It surely is worth the effort.

THE TWO SEAS

Summer tourists who, in increasing numbers, are going to the Holy Land are familiar with the two seas in that area. One is the Sea of Galilee and the other is the Dead Sea.

The Sea of Galilee was the scene of much of the public ministry of Jesus. Here he swam, fished, visited with his neighbors, instructed his Disciples in his way of life. From the shores of this sea he spoke to great multitudes of people in the late evening after the day's work was over. The heart of Jesus' ministry took place along the shores of Galilee.

These shores are still teeming with life. Villages and towns dot the lush shoreline. Fishermen in their boats still catch fish from the sparkling waters. Young people still bathe along the coast. Stores and shops are crowded with eager shoppers. Children play on the beaches and sheep and their shepherds drink of the fresh water.

From the north the river Jordan flows into the Sea of Galilee bringing its cool waters from the hill country. It flows out again into the Jordan valley to the south, giving up much of the water that it received.

Seventy miles south of the Sea of Galilee is the Dead Sea. It is ten miles wide and forty miles long, four times larger than the Sea of Galilee. But in these waters there are no fish, no birds, no insects on the surface of the water. There is no grass at the water's edge, no trees on the shoreline, no sheep coming down to drink, no villages, no people. Thirsty travelers from the desert dare not drink the waters.

What is the difference in these two seas?

Not the river Jordan. It empties practically the same amount of good water into both seas. Nor is it in the soil or the climate of the surrounding country.

Herein lies the great difference: The Sea of Galilee receives the refreshing waters and passes them on to the Jordan valley below. The Dead Sea receives the same refreshing waters but refuses to release them to the parched lands below.

The Sea of Galilee receives . . . and gives. The Dead Sea receives . . . and keeps.

The Sea of Galilee is teeming with life. The Dead Sea wears the shroud of death.

There are two seas in the Holy Land. One gives—and lives. The other hoards—and dies.

There are two kinds of people in the world. Some of them receive and give—to the United Fund, the neighbor in need, child welfare—and live! Others of them receive and keep—and die!

THE CROSS IS NOT AN ISOLATED EVENT

The most scandalous lie in history is the one told by prejudiced people who insist that the Jews crucified Christ. To be sure, He was crucified in Jerusalem, center of the Jewish nation. But that cross was no isolated event in history. It is contemporary, on the horizon of every man's life.

Golgotha is in the geography of the infinite and Calvary is in the calendar of the timeless. In a real sense all of humanity was at the foot at that cross. Some were participants, some were spectators, some among those who wept.

The Pharisees were there. They were the relgious technicians of their day. They strained gnats and swallowed camels, said their perfunctory prayers and robbed widows of their mites, insisted that they had a corner on all truth. We make no pleas for thought control but we do insist on the Lincolnian formula: "In essentials unity, in nonessentials liberty, in all things charity." But since Jesus didn't conform to their way of thinking, they nailed Him to a cross.

The sons of Annas, the high priest, were there. They doubled their profits at the expense of the poor by selling animals for sacrifice in atonement for sins. These fellows are still among us, bleeding the public every time they get a chance with no sense of responsibility for the common good. When someone suggests more bread for the starving they say, "Away with him."

The mob was there. A mob is an unthinking mass of people whose prejudice gets the better of them. When someone suggests restraint, the mob chants, "Crucify, crucify."

The indifferent were there. Some of them were simply caught in the crowd. They went where they were pushed, having nothing else to do.

Indifferent people don't bother about the principles involved. They just vote with the majority if, indeed, they vote at all.

The devoted were there. There were the three Marys, some of the faithful disciples and friends. They cried out—but in vain!

Don't you suppose that all of us were somehow at the feet of that cross?

GNATS AND CAMELS

Artists have probably unintentionally done violence to the portrait of the Man of Galilee. They have depicted him as a man of sorrows and acquainted with grief. But he was also a man of joy and acquainted with laughter. He said things that were positively funny, things that moved people to uproarious laughter.

Consider Jesus' story about straining at gnats and swallowing camels. The Pharisees in his day were very particular about what they ate. A group of Pharisees were in the sidewalk cafe at teatime and swarms of gnats were pestering them to death.

When one of the gnats loses its sense of direction and powerdives into the hot tea, the Pharisee methodically fishes out the drowned gnat. About this time a lumbering two-humped camel puts his nose into the man's mouth, kicks until the first lump is out of sight, then the second lump, until finally all you can see of the massive creature is two hind feet slipping down the Pharisaical esophagus.

What a marvelous way of driving home the point that men often make mountains out of petty things while they quietly consent to gross injustices.

Historically, we have strained gnats and swallowed camels. Constantine, the first so called Christian Emperor, saw the sign of the cross in the sky and adopted it as the sacred emblem of his armies.

In the name of God he went out to fight, brought back thousands of men, women and children as captives and sold them as slaves on the streets of Rome. Was this the way to follow the crucified Christ? I cannot believe it.

In Victorian England there was a law against playing the piano on Sunday, that being a day of meditation. Yet poor children were forced to labor in British mines twelve hours a day, seven days a week, often contracting tuberculosis before they were grown.

In Colonial New England there was a law against a man kissing his wife in public, while at the same time the citizens were hanging people who were found guilty of witchcraft. Straining gnats and swallowing camels indeed.

At the last count someone found out that we now have some three hundred different denominations in the United States. Why so many when all claim Christ Lord of Lords? In most instances—piffles! It is about time the people of God began marching together against the forces that would destroy us, our sons and our sons' sons.

THE STRANGER

There he stood in the midst of them, curiously alone. He wore unshapely shoes, a threadbare coat, baggy trousers, a battered hat pulled low over sullen, disappointed eyes.

His name was Ted Warren—but the name meant nothing to anyone. He was alone in a vast sea of humanity, and on Christmas Eve, at that. As he glanced across the street he saw the twinkling lights on a Christmas tree and his lips curled in bitterness.

Deep pangs of hunger had driven him to the soup line. That wavering black column of humanity was slowly moving to the door where warm soup was being given to the hungry.

Ted Warren particularly noticed the man in front of him. His clothing was unusual, made of material strangely homespun and coarse. He turned toward Ted, a radiant smile enveloping his face.

"Colder tonight, isn't it," Ted said. Then the stranger began to speak, measuring every word.

"This food for the hungry is a beautiful thing," the stranger said. At the sound of his voice Ted found a quickening thrill, for it was a voice soft and deep, the sure voice of a kind and learned man.

"Been out of work very long?" asked the stranger.

"Quite a long time," Ted said. "You see I'm just an untrained laborer and in the last few months I have had very few jobs. I seem to have lost everything worthwhile."

"Everything?" asked the stranger. "You are young and strong and here is food for you."

"Charity," cried Ted. "Charity is bitter in my mouth."

But the stranger looked serious. "Do you not like that which is offered freely? Some have plenty, and of that plenty, they give. Is that not good?"

"You don't understand. I have suffered," said Ted.

"Suffered?" asked the stranger.

As they ate their hot soup, Ted noticed familiar lines in the stranger's face.

"Haven't I seen—don't I know you?" Ted stammered.

But apparently the stranger had not heard. The hand that held the soup spoon was brown and on the back of it was an ugly scar.

"What did you do before you came to this soup line?" Ted asked.

"I was once a carpenter, then a teacher. But many of my teachings are almost forgotten."

Ted studied the stranger's face—dark eyes under a scarred forehead.

"I know you" Ted said.

"Do you?" the stranger replied with his eyes glistening. "I'm glad."

"I must be going" said the stranger. "It gives me joy to see the hungry fed, to see people helping people. This is like a birthday feast."

"Birthday?" questioned Ted.

"Yes, you see tomorrow is my birthday," the stranger said.

As he left the room there was a brightness that had not been there before. For wherever there is kindness, there is the rebirth of Christ.

HE WROTE THE SCRIPT

From Paul's letters to the Galatians we know the familiar words "Be not deceived, God is not mocked, for whatsoever a man sows, that will he also reap."

These words remind us of an ancient proverb which reads "The mills of God grind slowly, but they grind exceedingly small." Everywhere we look we find evidence of this truth. Farmers who plant corn—given rain, sunshine and fertile soil—are sure to reap corn at harvest time. The universal law of sowing and reaping is constantly being taken for granted. People who break the law of the land usually ultimately reap the results. Thieves, drunkards and murderers all have their rewards, according to the seeds they sow.

The U.S. Congress, as far as the records indicate, has never gotten around to suggesting the repeal of a single one of the Ten Commandments. Obviously some of them have broken one, two or more of them, but they had enough sense not to brag about it. The fact is, individuals do not break the laws of God. They only break themselves. God's laws are as eternal as the stars above us.

Some years ago Arturo Toscanini, the Italian conductor of the NBC Symphony Orchestra, went to London, England, as guest conductor of the London Symphony Orchestra in the presentation of Beethoven's Ninth Symphony.

Toscanini, a perfectionist, drove the musicians to near exhaustion in his effort to present a flawless masterpiece in music. When the time came for the concert the music hall was filled to overflowing with distinguished music lovers both from Europe and America. And, as expected, the two hundred musicians actually did give a flawless presentation of Beethoven's Ninth Symphony. A dozen times the curtain was raised because of the audience response.

When the curtain was lowered for the last time, Toscanini respectfully asked each musician to remain quietly in his place. Then Toscanini, looking around at the musicians, asked the question "Who are you?" Then after a long pause, he said, "You are nothing!" "Who am I?" "I am nothing!" Another pause, and then, "Beethoven is everything. He wrote the script!"

This is God's world by right of creation. He wrote the script!

WHAT'S THE GOOD NEWS?

Lloyd C. Douglas, author of such novels as *The Magnificent Obsession*, and *The Robe*, used to visit a little old man who gave violin lessons in his home town. One day he walked into the old man's studio and, by way of greeting, said, "What's the good news today?"

The old gentleman put down his violin, stepped over to a tuning fork suspended from a silk cord, struck it a resounding blow with a rubber mallet, returned to his friend and said, "That, my friend, is the good news today. That note was A. It was A yesterday and it will be A tomorrow and a thousand years from now. The soprano upstairs warbles off-key, the tenor next door flats his high notes and the piano cross the hall is out of tune. There are noises all around me but when that mallet hits that tuning fork the tone is always A."

That was the old man's idea of the good news in his day.

And it ought to be our idea of the good news in this day of confusion. It behooves us to remember that, despite change on every hand, there are some truths which are as eternal as the heavens above.

In Connelly's play *Green Pastures* the angel Gabriel is sent by God down to earth to see how the people are getting along. His report is quite blunt: "Lord, there ain't nothing fastened down there any more. Everything that ain't nailed down is coming loose."

And that's the way it seems in our world right now. But it isn't so. The law of sowing and reaping has not been repealed. The laws against murder, theft and dishonesty have not been repealed. The Ten Commandments haven't been abolished . . . though many people have wrecked their lives on the assumption they were not true.

The simple fact is that man does not break the eternal laws of God. G. K. Chesterton said there was once a man who disbelieved in the law of gravity. To prove his disbelief he walked off the edge of a cliff. But he did not break the law of gravity . . . he only broke himself.

Some laws change. In puritanical New England it used to be against the law to play the piano in a private residence on Sunday. There was a law against a man kissing his wife in public. Human progress is recorded in the making of new laws and the repealing of obsolete ones. But the moral laws of God do not change with the passing time. The Ten Commandments are not true because they are in the Bible. They are in the Bible because they are true. God's laws were established with the establishment of the universe. And that's the good news . . . until the end of time.

IS ANYBODY OUT THERE?

Since the days of Adam and Eve, men have observed the wonders of the world beneath them, the movements of the sun around them, the millions of stars above them, and have asked the age-old question: "Is anybody out there?"

There are those who have peered into the darkness, listened in the stillness, looked into the silent depths of space and said, "There is no God out there."

But the most significant step in history was made when Jesus unveiled the face of God and taught us to think of him as "father." Granted, it is a human word but what other words do humans have?

Sir James Jeans thinks of God as more like a great thought then a great machine. Scientist A. S. Eddington writes, "We have found a strange footprint on the shores of the unknown."

The word "father" is the key word in understanding the nature of God. If God is father, he is not almighty in the sense that he can do anything he wishes. He is limited by his fatherhood. He gave to his children freedom and doesn't change his mind.

But he is no absentee landlord. When Jesus preached, he reminded us that the world of nature about him was the expression of the father's mind. No blade of grass grew without God's care. No sparrow ever fell from the sky without the father's notice. He said, "My Father worketh."

Furthermore, when Jesus said "father" he did not say God was an almighty king or almighty ruler, but an almighty father. An earthly father must withhold power—physical and mental—and wait with infinite patience until his children grow up and learn what it means to be a mature person.

When we hear people say that, the world being in the mess that it is now in, we can expect God to take over, cast the wicked into perdition and save the remnant.

What do we mean by taking over? Take over the struggles by which we grow? Remove the risks? Make human beings who cannot sin? The almighty father must wait for the free cooperation of the human will. He himself gave us freedom to disobey.

Finally, if God is the father, he not only works and waits, but seeks. We talk as though he were hiding somewhere. Probably the shoe is on the other foot. He seeks us.

The only time God is described as running was when his younger son, tired of the hogpen, started home. And when the father saw him, he ran and fell on his neck. That is God, said Jesus. Someone out there is calling my name.

IS IT A GOOD DAY OR A BAD DAY?

Lin Yutang, brilliant Chinese philosopher, tells a fascinating story about an old farmer who had a wife and one son . . . and a horse. He was the envy of all the other farmers because he had a horse to do the heavy plowing. It was not long, however, before the horse ran away and could not be found. The neighbors came to console him in his great loss but the old man asked them: "How do you know that this is a bad day?"

Several days later the old farmer looked out to find that his horse had returned . . . bringing nine other horses with him. The neighbors returned to congratulate him on his good fortune. He could easily be the richest man in the community. But the old man asked: "How do you know that this is a good day?"

In the days that followed, his eighteen-year-old son was out in the corral grooming the horses when one of them kicked him and broke his leg. Again, the neighbors grathered around to console the father because of the accident of his son. He asked them: "How do you know that this is a bad day?"

Some months later a Chinese war lord came through the country conscripting able-bodied young men for his army. Obviously the young man with the broken leg could not go. So the neighbors came to congratulate the farmer because his son did not have to go to war. As you would expect the farmer asked: "How do you know this is a good day?"

This could go on forever but the point of the story is that you never know whether it is a good day or a bad day until you and God get through with it. We assume, for instance, that it is a good day when we strike it rich and a bad day when we suffer financial reverses.

Yet I have known men of affluence who will admit that their days of prosperity brought them the greatest tragedies of their lives. You never know if it is a good or a bad day until you learn how to handle it.

We assume it is a good day when we are healthy and a bad day when health fails. But I have known people who admitted they did not know the value of good health until they were arrested in midstream with a prolonged heart attack.

We assume it is a good day when we succeed and a bad day when we fail. But I am quite sure that the many defeats of Abraham Lincoln before his presidency made of him one of the great presidents in history.

It was a bad day when Jesus was crucified on a hill outside Jerusalem. But after God got through with it, it became a day of hope and glory. No particular twenty-four hours in a day is good or bad in itself. It has always depended on what you and God do with it.

GOD IS IN ULTIMATE CONTROL

For some time I watched a TV program in which unusual people, some of whom were handicapped, performed incredible feats. I have made a little list of incredibles of my own that may be of interest.

   • It is incredible to me that the universe just happened by accident. If I were to throw a bucket of letters into the air, it is incredible to assume that any of them falling to the floor would make a complete, meaningful sentence. Nevertheless, the way the cells of the human embryo are determined—some to make nerves, some bones, some teeth, some brains, each in its appointed place and time—convinces me that there is a mind behind the universe.

• It is incredible to me that my sense of values is all wrong. I think love is better than hate, kindness is better than cruelty, humility is better than pride and peace is better than war.

• It is incredible to me that the creative mind of God has no personality; that God is "it" rather than "he;" a thing rather than a person.

• It is incredible to me that this creative God has no purpose for humanity. If I plan for the well-being of my children, can God do less?

• It is incredible to me that Jesus Christ never lived or that he was hopelessly mistaken when he claimed a unique relationship with God.

• It is incredible to me that man does not survive death. The nature of God, the nature of man and the rationality of the universe would all be indicted if man does not survive. As the babe in the womb has eyes and ears for life's beginning, so all men have qualities that endure beyond death.

• It is incredible to me that the creator of the universe can finally be defeated. Omnipotence does not mean that everything that happens is God's will. It does mean that, despite human weakness, we can be sure that God, who put the stars in place, is in ultimate control.

ONE LONELY MAN

The most significant thing about Jesus was that he was born a normal baby, grew up as a normal child and lived, until his crucifixion, as a normal individual. He was vastly different, to be sure, because he was sinless. But the striking thing about him was that he was so much like us.

When God wanted to reveal Himself to the world he didn't appoint a committee, pass new laws, shake the stars or send an earthquake. He simply sent one lonely man to live among us.

Here, in some detail, is what James Francis said of Jesus:

"He never wrote a book. He never held an office. He never owned a home. He never went to college. He never traveled two hundred miles from where he was born.

"He had no credentials but himself. Yet all the armies that ever marched, all the navies that were ever built, all the parliaments that ever sat, all the kings that ever reigned, put together, have not affected the life of man as powerfully as that one solitary life."

In these days of mass movements we need to recover the sense of the value of the individual person. Someone who has more time than I have, found out that it took 70,276 drops of water to fill a gallon bucket. And when the bucket was full, it was a bucket full of water instead of a bucket full of drops. Each drop lost its individuality in the mass. So man seems to lose his individuality among the masses.

But this is not really so. The person is and has always been of utmost importance. Behind every progressive movement in the history of humanity there is an individual person. Behind the prison reform movement of the eighteenth century was John Howard of Bedford, England.

Behind the movement to establish hospitals for the insane in America was William Tuke, the Quaker. Behind the worldwide Boy Scout movement was Sir William Baden-Powell. Behind the 4-H Clubs throughout the United States was Jesse Shambaugh of Iowa. Behind every forward move for racial integration in America was Martin Luther King, Jr.

In the open country out of Geneva, Switzerland, there is a beautiful church with no lighting facilities. It was given to the community by a well-to-do benefactor with the understanding that no lighting fixtures would ever be installed. All the people who worshipped here were asked to bring their own candle at the evening services. If one segment of the church was dark it was because some of the worshippers failed to let their lights shine.

Every person among us counts. This is the gospel according to the lonely Man of Galilee.

HEART TROUBLE

Sometime ago I remember reading a quote from one of Bob Hope's monologues, which was something like this: "Today my heart beat 86,400 times, my blood traveled 168 thousand miles, I breathed 28,794 times, I inhaled 438 cubic feet of air, I ate 3 pounds of food, drank 2.9 pounds of liquid, perspired 1.43 pints, gave off 85 degrees of heat, generated 450 tons of energy, spoke 4,800 words, moved 750 major muscles, my nails grew .00056 inches, my hair grew .01714 inches and I exercised 7 million brain cells. No wonder I'm tired."

I will not take responsibility for Bob Hope's figures, but I can understand why human beings get tired. The organ no larger than our double fists called the heart does a tremendous amount of work in the course of the day.

Yet it is amazing the amount of work some people do each day. Evidently tired hearts result, not simply from the amount of work done, but from the spirit in which the work is done. Those people who seem to be happy in their work return home with more energy and more enthusiasm than those who think of their jobs as sheer drudgery.

In advancing age, arteries often lose their elasticity, become hardened, putting unusual strain on the heart. Psychiatrists tell us that when we maintain cynical, surly and sour attitudes about life we hasten the hardening artery process. Hardened arteries frequently follow hardened dispositions.

Evidently some people die of broken hearts. Years ago I had a very good friend who lost his wife when she was in her early forties. She was deeply loved by her husband and her two sons.

The husband blamed her death on God. "God took her from me," he said. I tried desperately to remind him that God suffered her to be taken. Did not God lose his beloved son, Jesus? But my friend was bitter, even cursed God. Two years later, he died of a congestive heart attack. He had lost the will to live.

Much of our heart troubles can be cured if we keep our hearts warm, live thankfully, labor leisurely and love family and friends lavishly. Any person who has lived as long as I have has had his troubles. But I keep reminding myself that I have $2 million eyes, a pair of $1 million ears, $1 million appetite—and I am a millionaire—without the million.

'IF YOU HAD THREE DAYS TO SEE'

The headline of this article is taken from one written forty years ago by the blind but brilliant Helen Keller. She had been asked, if she could be given sight for just three days, what would she look for?

She said that on the first day she would call on those dear friends such as Ann Sullivan Macy who had made her own life so enriching. She would see in their faces the outward evidence of the beauty of life within them.

She also would look into the face of a little baby and catch a vision of the innocent beauty which preceeds the individual's awareness of the conflicts which come in later life. She would want to see the many books which had been read to her revealing the beauty of human life.

In the afternoon and evening of the first day, she would take a long walk into the woods and bathe her eyes in the beauty of the world's natural wonders.

On the second day Ms. Keller said she would arise with the dawn and see for herself the thrilling miracle by which night is transformed into day. She would go to the museums to see the condensed history of the earth, the animals and the races of men pictured in their native environment.

She would later visit famous art galleries so the magnificent world of painting would be opened to her. She would spend an evening in a theatre or movie observing the characters which reflect life on the streets from day to day.

Ms. Keller said she would like to spend the third day strolling down Fifth Avenue, New York. She would want to see the vivid colors and styles of the womens' dresses amid the throng of people. She would want to take a tour of the city visiting in the slums, the prisons, the factories, the public parks where people play.

She also would want to see the people who were poor, the rich, the happy, the miserable and the suffering. At midnight on the third day, Ms. Keller would go back into her world of darkness again. Only then would she realize just how much her eyes had not seen.

Helen Keller in her blindness has taught many of us how to be grateful for all five of the senses with which we are endowed. It is too bad that so many of us have eyes that seldom see beauty, ears that seldom hear great truths and fingers that are insensitive to the cry of the unfortunate.

A TALE OF TWO POPES

The Catholic Church is fortunate in having as its leader such a friendly, outgoing person as the beloved Pope John Paul II. Millions of people throughout the world fervently prayed for his speedy recovery from the bullet wounds of a would-be assassin.

Perhaps the only other Pope who was equally as popular was Pope John XXIII, who was elected in 1958 and served until his death in 1963. Pope John XXIII became the head of the Roman Catholic Church, almost by sheer accident. He was one of 13 children whose parents were sharecroppers in Italy.

As a boy of 12, he did a man's work. In his preparation for the priesthood, he proved himself to be a prodigious scholar, well versed in history, theology and philosophy.

He preached the gospel of peace, justice and mercy to all mankind, regardless of race, creed or nationality. He pointed out that the churches of the world were overlooking their responsibilities to the impoverished, the disinherited, the starving masses of mankind.

When the bishops met in Rome in 1958, they chose Cardinal Roncalli of Venice, who took the name of John XXIII. The bishops really thought they were electing a tired, 70-year-old man who would serve as interim pope while they could get their political machinery organized.

Pope John XXIII fooled them. He became one of the great popes in history.

Tradition was broken from the beginning of his leadership. He called for a Vatican Council to meet in Rome and personally invited religious leaders from all nations to meet with him and discuss such problems as world peace, food for the poor, and justice for all men regardless of race, creed or color.

He had a saving sense of humor. Once, when attending a banquet, he found himself seated by an elegant lady wearing an extremely low-neck dress. During the course of the meal, he invited her to share an apple with him. When she demurred, he insisted. "Please take it; only after Eve ate the apple did she become aware that she was not properly dressed."

Both Pope John Paul and Pope John XXIII are my kind of people.

ON BEING RUN RAGGED AND LOVING IT

Several summers ago, our little granddaughter Alex, then eight years of age, flew down from Philadelphia for a visit. While her two grandmothers confiscated most of her time, they did manage to allow me the privilege of taking her to Six Flags for an afternoon and evening visit.

We started out immediately after lunch to beat the crowds and discovered that several thousand others had done the same thing. We parked our car somewhere over in an adjoining county and walked a long mile to what we thought was the front gate. Too late we discovered it was an "exit only." We had to walk another mile before arriving at the main entrance.

By this time Alex had established a gait of travel somewhat slower than that of a frightened antelope, and I began to worry about heat exhaustion. In sharp contrast to my body weaknesses, Alex seemed to have only one. She wanted to ride everything that moved. Merry-go-rounds, ferris wheels, drive-yourself jalopies and hollowed-out boatrides down steep chutes ending in unholy baptisms of water wetting our clothes to the skin.

The more exhausted I became, the more exuberant Alex became. She quickly recuperated her energy by eating. The many places to dine were quite attractive and you can get well-balanced meals at prices any Arabian sheik can afford. Dining is "gracious" because that is the word nonswearing people use when they learn that hot dogs without mustard cost $1.49 each and soft drinks in four-ounce cups go for 79 cents plus tax. What would I give for an appetite like Alex's.

As we stumbled out of Six Flags at eight in the evening, Alex said, "Granddad, we forgot to ride the head-over-heels roller coaster." I lifted my eyes up over the electric lights to the stars above and prayed with all earnestness: "Thank you, God, for making little grandchildren and dumb granddads who still think they can keep up with them." After all, wherever we go we find only the fun we bring with us. We never have to check that at the gates.

LATE BLOOMERS

I hear it on good authority that a distinguished president of an Eastern university who also is Phi Beta Kappa made a speech extoling the virtues of being in the bottom 90 percent of the graduating class instead of the top 10 percent.

The speech came fifty years too late for me but I surely could have used it when I was in college making 70 in history, 65 in French and 60 in algebra. I have nothing whatever against the top 10 percent (except envy) but I am glad someone has finally said a good word for the bottom 90 percent with whom I am much better acquainted.

The distinguished president said the college community had put too much emphasis on precocity, those receiving the highest grades. He dropped the comforting thought that many geniuses whose average grade was 99.5 or better had frequently shot their last intellectual wad and possibly might never fire again.

He said we should pay more attention to "late bloomers" who come on slowly in the spring but, ere the snow flies, they proliferate into gorgeous roses as large as sunflowers. Play it again Sam, play it again.

I remember the algebra teacher who flunked me, saying, "No one who failed in my class has ever amounted to much in life." If I could speak to her again I would say, "Miss Minerva, you are all wet. Your theories are out of date. I am not a moron despite my low grades. I am simply a late bloomer just like the president said. I may yet be the great white hope of civilization."

What a boon this good news will be to a great host of parents. They have literally agonized over the low grades of their children, have been troubled by every report card, distressed but not despaired, cast down but not destroyed. Now they can lift up their heads and shout, "My children are late bloomers! There is still hope!"

There is every higher authority for late bloomers other than the words of the university president. The good Book says, "Be not weary in well doing for in due season you shall reap if you faint not." In the world of sports the word is: "The game is never over until the last whistle has blown." Down in Comanche County where I grew up they said: "It is the last lick that splits the log."

DOES GOD MATTER?

There is an old Danish story that tells about a spider that slid down a single filament of web from a rafter in the barn and made its home on a lower level. The web was so woven that it caught more flies than the spider could possibly use each day. Consequently the spider grew sleek and fat and prospered. One afternoon while the spider was wandering about its premises it saw the single thread that stretched up in the dark, unseen above its web. Being a practical spider it said, "That surely is a useless thread." So he snapped it. But the web collapsed and spider and web were soon trodden under the feet of the barnyard animals.

The curse of modern life is man's decision that he can get along quite well without God, that God does not matter, that man is the master of things. The most sinister thing about these hectic days in which we live is that life is organized around man, rather than around God. When we cut the thread that leads us to the great Unknown and Unseen, we fall on our faces. The history of humanity is largely the story of man trying to push God off His throne and get on it himself. The Caesars of Rome, denying God, made of themselves a god. In our own day, Hitler sought to rewrite the Bible, deleting the phrases which extolled the virtues of the Jews, in order that he might destroy them. Denying God, we make of ourselves gods.

How queer some of our expressions are. We talk about breaking God's laws. Can a 160-pound man break the laws governing the limitless Universe? Nonsense. A man who jumps out a ten-story building doesn't break the law of gravity. He demonstrates it. We don't break God's laws. We break ourselves against them. God's moral laws are as real as His physical laws.

I think it was H. G. Wells who said, "If there is no God, nothing matters. If there is a God, nothing else matters." I do remember reading the words of Professor Toynbee, the great historian of our day, who, at the end of a ten-volume historical survey, said: "The entire story of man on earth has no meaning at all except a religious meaning. There is no hope except in the vast increase of spiritual religion." He points out the fact that history records the rise of twenty-one separate civilizations. Of the twenty-one, fourteen have already disappeared. They were instruments which God could no longer use. God did not destroy them! The absence of God did that. Will that be our fate?

PEOPLE THE MEASURE OF GREATNESS

What is your idea of the greatest city in the world? Washington? Moscow? New York? London? Athens? Tokyo? Rome? A person's choice depends on what he looks for in greatness.

Businessmen would list their choice in terms of business centers. Artists would choose the city where the greatest amount of art is found. Historians would name cities with chief historical interest. Sportsmen would choose cities where they could participate in a variety of sports events.

Sometime ago a large group of school children was asked to draw up a list of those people they considered the greatest characters in history. They were also asked to list the towns or cities in which these renowned people were born. Take a good look at this list: Dole, Hodgenville, Genoa, Bridges Creek, Boston, Florence, Domremy, Athens, Mainz and Blantrye. Do you recognize any of them?

From a cradle in Dole, France, came Louis Pasteur, chemist,

discoverer of bacilli causing many communicable disease. He developed curative treatment of anthrax, hydrophobia, etc. From Hodgenville, Kentucky, came Abraham Lincoln, whose memorial in Washington, D.C. attracts millions of visitors and whose life became a heroic guide for many.

From Genoa, Italy, came Christopher Columbus, discoverer of the New World. From Bridges Creek, Virginia, came George Washington, father of our country. From Boston came Benjamin Franklin, inventor and philosopher. From Florence, Italy, came Florence Nightingale, founder of the modern nursing movement.

From Domremy, France, came Joan of Arc and her will to resist human slavery. From Athens came Socrates, wisest among the Greeks. Out of Mainz, Germany, came Johann Gutenberg, and thus the movable-type printing press. And from Blantrye, Scotland, came David Livingstone, who initiated the International Missionary movement that continues to change the worth today.

The true measure of a city is the quality of manhood it produces. To be sure, we are proud of our factories, banks and business enterprises. But our primary responsibility is the building of a city in which the environment is conducive to growth of wholesome, healthy, sober and honest young people with such character as has made America great. Our chief asset is *people*.

MEANINGLESSNESS

An average of about twenty-two thousand Americans will take their own lives within the next twelve months. Every four minutes someone somewhere in the United States attempts suicide. And the tendency to self-destruction is growing. Suicide ranks as the eleventh leading cause of death. There are many reasons for this despair: the sudden loss of financial security; marital difficulties; loss of health; or a combination of things too numerous to mention. If I were to try to put my finger on the one word describing the mental attitude of the suicide victim it would be . . . meaninglessness. People come to the conclusion that life simply isn't worth the effort.

The tendency to self-destruction is as old as human history. One of our contemporary philosophers has said, "Man prattles about his kinship with the archangels while, in his faith, he digs for ground-nuts." Lord Byron said, "Man is a degraded mass of animated dust." Schiller said it like this: "Man originates in muck, sits in muck, makes muck and, in the end, returns to muck." Theodore Dreiser, American novelist said, "As far as being a free, independent spirit, nonsense. As I see it, man walks a wholly meaningless course. I catch no meaning from what I have seen." Rabelais, the French satirist, said upon his deathbed, "Draw the curtain. The farce is ended." Such concepts inevitably lead to frustration, futility, meaninglessness.

Is life worth living? It depends upon the person. Man is given a choice. He can live a totally meaningless life. Or he can make it meaningful . . . to himself, to others, to God. I believe that man is the most valuable creature in the universe. More valuable than the Sistine Madonna was Raphael, the artist; more valuable than the yellow copy of a Shakespearean play was Shakespeare. Since I am a person, I have the capacity to be of great value.

Furthermore, since other people have been of great value to me, I in turn can be of great value to other people. Behind every good thing is a good person. Behind the Red Cross was Clara Barton. Behind the Boy Scout movement was William Baden-Powell. If I expect to have friends, I must be a friend to someone else. There is no other person in the world exactly like me. (Lucky world.) And if I don't do the job that God has for me to do . . . it won't get done!

'FIFTY-SEVEN PENNIES'

It happened almost a hundred years ago in Philadelphia, the city of brotherly love. A young Baptist minister, Russell H. Conwell, was called to be the shepherd of a small flock of people in one of the poorest areas of the city.

Because of the winsomeness of his personality and the time-liness of his sermons, the little church could not possibly accommodate the people who wanted to attend the services. Hattie Wiatt was one of the children who wanted to come to Sunday School, but could not get in for lack of room. Bitterly disappointed, she began to cry.

When Dr. Conwell saw the little girl in tears, he picked her up and carried her in the church on his shoulders, telling her they would eventually have a church large enough for all the people. Hattie went home and told her parents that she was going to save her money and help Dr. Conwell build a church. Her parents humored her in the idea and gave her the opportunity to earn a few pennies each week, and she dropped them in her piggie bank.

Hattie was a lovable little girl, liked by all who knew her. But in the course of a few weeks she became seriously ill and, after a lingering illness, passed away. At the funeral, the father gave Dr. Conwell the fifty-seven cents found in the piggie bank. When the minister told the members of the church about the pennies, they voted unanimously to buy land for a larger church. They bought ten thousand dollars worth of land with only fifty-seven cents as a down payment. Within a year, inspired by Hattie Wiatt's initial gift, the people paid off the indebtedness and prepared to erect a church building seating three thousand persons and costing more than $100,000.

In the course of the years, the members of the Temple Baptist Church were as good as their word. Furthermore, the congregation was largely responsible for the founding of Temple University, which has a present enrollment of about twenty thousand students, and Temple Hospital, which serves thousands of patients in an impoverished area of the city.

And it all began with a beautiful dedicated little girl and "fifty-seven pennies."

DOUBTING OUR DOUBTS

In the vocabulary of religion the word "doubt" has an offensive significance. In religious circles the great word is faith. Yet in any given period in history the great servants of mankind have distinguished themselves by challenging falsehoods and crying, "I doubt that."

Five hundred years ago in the realm of science it was believed that the Earth was flat and that the sun moved around it. But Copernicus and Galileo, despite overwhelming opposition, had the courage to say, "I doubt that." The fact is that every scientific advance has started with skepticism. In the realm of religion we must have faith in God, in Christ, in prayer, in the universe. But if we think we can achieve great faith without exercising our God-given capacity to doubt, we are oversimplifying the problem.

Jesus himself was a great doubter. He saw men making long prayers, observing rigid Sabbath rules, dietary laws, sacrificing animals in atonement for sin and cried out, "It was said of them in old time . . . but I say unto you."

We sing praises to great believers and we should. But we dare not withhold our unpayable debt to the brave doubters who saved the day with their courageous disbeliefs. Sturdy faith always comes out of the struggle with doubt. The Bible is a book of faith filled with the struggle of people who wrestle with their doubts. Listen to our Lord on Calvary! Quoting the Twenty-third Psalm, amid his agony, Jesus cried, "My God, my God, why hast thou forsaken me?" Profound faith is hammered out on the anvil of doubt.

Great believers wrestle with their disbeliefs until, at last, they begin to doubt their doubts. When it was first suggested that a steamboat could cross the Atlantic, a man wrote a book proving it could not be done. But when the first steamboat made the crossing, it carried that book. The author should have carried his doubts further until he doubted his doubts.

You have doubts about God? Wrestle with them. Look through a microscope or a telescope and see the magnificent plan of nature. If there is a plan, is there not a planner? If there is a creation, is there not a creator? Call him by any name you want. Jesus called him Father.

I'VE GOT A LITTLE LIST

I recently was reminiscing with an old friend of mine from the ministry. We were discussing the small number of people in the churches we had served who had given us the most trouble. To our surprise, the lists were remarkably similar.

The first person on the list was the highly loquacious church member who was always recalling at length and with warm emotion, how much better everything was when Dr. Demosthenes, our predecessor, was pastor. "Ah, those were the days. [Sigh] He packed them in like sardines; standing room only at every service."

The next person on the list was Brother P. Nurious, the pillar of the church. He had made a pledge to the church thirty years ago and had seen no reason to change it since. He felt that the Old Testament commandment not to remove the ancient landmark also applied to an ancient pledge. For thirty years he felt himself to be an emblem of hope in a needy world—for five dollars a week.

Neither of us dared to overlook Mrs. Gotrocks who lived in the brownstone mansion on top of the hill. She was a lovely person, but became quite irritated when the pastor didn't visit her home at least once a month. She had not revised her thinking since the horse and buggy days when the pastor worked his feet so fast visiting, that he had little time to work his head.

Nor could we ever forget that Trustee, the Watchdog of the Treasury. He would block any project for which the cold cash was not in his hands. He used to say, "My mother taught me never to buy anything unless I had the cash in my hands." And every day proved to be Mother's Day with him.

Yet, despite such negativism, the living church moves on.

KEEPING THE FUNNY BONE WELL OILED

Somewhere around the region of your elbow is the funny bone. If you insist on locating it, try cracking your elbow on a table top. It is one part of the anatomy we ought to keep well oiled and in good working order.

If I were so bold as to suggest an additional biblical beatitude, it would be: "Blessed is the man with a well oiled funny bone for humor hath great redemptive powers."

Does not God himself have a sense of humor? "He who sits in the heavens laughs." (Ps. 2:4) It seems that when he made some of us he was laughing out loud. Man is the only creature that God ever made who has the capacity both to laugh and to work. Both are essential elements in human history.

Happy is the man who has the capacity to laugh at himself. My good friend, John Doe, somehow conceived the idea that he knew absolutely everything worth knowing. He assumed his judgment was superior to the total judgment of his employees.

Then after a series of dumb stunts bordering on the catastrophic, John sat back in his swivel chair with his shriveled brain in his shriveled head and had a good look at himself. What he saw made him laugh. Acknowledging his mistakes, he arose from his chair, a wiser and a more humble man.

Sally Doe, John's wife, had been told by some old fossil that she was not only brilliant but beautiful. Susceptible to such flattery, she became contemptuous of those whom she considered less fortunate. Becoming thoroughly miserable herself. She also made those about her miserable.

Then one morning after a sleepless night and before the application of powder, mascara, eye shadow, and lipstick, she took a good look at herself in the mirror. She laughed. And that one chuckle saved her from an otherwise devastating disposition and a critical attitude toward others.

Happy is the man who can laugh at his troubles.

Someone said the reason Jesus associated with sinners so much was because he didn't like the company of the sour saints. Forty years ago, Will Rogers said, "I never met a man I didn't like." And I don't suppose anyone ever met Will Rogers who didn't like him. Keep your funny bone well oiled.

MAKE A FRIEND OF YOUR FEARS

When I was a small boy I lived in mortal fear of going to hell. Like most of you, I learned to pray—

> *Now I lay me down to sleep*
> *I pray the Lord my soul to keep*
> *If I should die before I wake*
> *I pray the Lord my soul to take.*

That third line didn't help a ten-year-old kid to sleep soundly. I was actually afraid I would wake up . . . dead.

The traveling evangelists who came to our town didn't help me overcome fear either. I shook hands with several of them simply because they scared me stiff. I shall never forget the eloquent speaker who said he was afraid of God . . . afraid that if he told a lie God would strike him dead. It seems to me that fear is the least valuable motive for the encouragement of Christian conduct. Is not the joy of the Christian life its own reward? Should we not love God simply for the joy of it?

Let's note some of the positive uses of fear.

Fear is a stimulus to knowledge. Fear of the unknown stimulates us to learn. Primitive man wanted to know what caused the death of his loved ones. So modern medicine was born.

Fear is a spur to action. The fear of political and religious slavery on the part of our ancestors spurred them to launch out on the Mayflower and endure the rugged winters of New England. It prompted them to pen their signatures to the Declaration of Independence on peril of their lives. The fear of poverty spurs us to work and wisely invest our savings. The fear of illness spurs us to observe the laws of health.

Fear, constructively used, is a force for righteousness. I am not now and never have been afraid of God. I don't believe God sends people to hell. But I am afraid of the absence of God. That, in itself, is . . . hell.

WHO AM I?

Some years ago at an American Legion convention in Ohio there was a man who was a victim of amnesia. Taking advantage of a short pause in the program the man rushed up to the microphone on stage and asked, "Does anyone here know who I am?" The poor fellow had lost all contact with his past life, did not know his name, where he lived, where he worked, whether or not he had a family. He was desperate for some acquaintance to tell him who he was, link him to his past life.

It is most important for a person to understand something of the value of his life. If we ever do lose our civilization the chances are it will be because we have adopted a low estimate of human personality. The Psalmist had a high concept of man when he said that God had created him "little lower than the angels." Consider these factors in assessing value to the person:

Man is the only creature of God who can say these two little words: "I am." Man possesses self-consciousness; he is aware of himself in time; he remembers yesterday, is aware of the present, concerned about the future. An astronomer once said, "Astronomically speaking, man is the essence of insignificance." But a philosopher answered him saying, "Astronomically speaking, man is the astronomer."

Man is the only creature of God who can say these two little words, "I think." To be sure, one can train his dog or horse to respond to his commands. But man can think in terms of abstract ideas, can record the results of his thinking in a book and put it in the library for posterity.

Man is the only creature of God who can say "I believe." We are surrounded by our creeds, both religious and political. We reassert our faith in the spirit of democracy every time we pledge allegiance to the flag.

Man is the only creature of God who can say "I ought." Normal man is born with a sense of moral oughtness. He cannot destroy little babies, as can an alligator, unless he is mentally deranged.

Man is the only creature of God who can say "I will." Dr. W. E. Hocking, formerly of Harvard, said that "man is the only creature whom God has allowed to finish his own life." As Shakespeare said, a man's future is not in his stars, but in himself. No wonder the Psalmist said, "Thou hast created man a little lower than the angels."

"THANK YOU, SIR"

In all probability the two most important words in the English language are, "Thank you." Sometime ago while in New York City I dropped into a department store and paid spot cash for a fifty-cent handkerchief. When I started to leave the clerk said, "Thank you, sir; it is a pleasure to wait on you." I was so astonished that I turned to her and said, "I've been here twenty-four hours and you are the first person who has said 'thank you' to me since my arrival."

I suppose we are all guilty of failure to say "thank you" at times. A postal employee in Washington was asked to study the mail that came to the dead-letter office during the thirty days before Christmas. Among the thousands of letters addressed to Santa Claus, all of them asked for the things they needed. But in the thirty days after Christmas there was only one letter addressed to Santa saying, "Thank you."

A business executive was telling me of a young man, only ten years out of school, who had just been promoted to general manager of his million-dollar enterprise. "How did it happen?" I asked. "There were many things," he said, "that entered into his situation but his chief asset is that he never fails to say, 'Thank you, sir'. Everyone appreciates him because he appreciates everyone."

Sincere use of these words would redeem many homes that are now being wrecked. A husband who expresses thanks for his wife and children, a mother who is grateful for the kindesses extended her, children expressing gratitude for parents—these magic words of thanks are the cement that holds the foundation of the home together.

Thanksgiving Day is just around the corner and obviously you can't cultivate the habit of giving thanks for your blessings in a single day. But if you spend an hour during the morning writing notes of thanks or speaking words of gratitude to those who have been helpful to you, it will be the best Thanksgiving you ever had.

Then you can make a high resolve to let no man or woman do you a good turn without giving an honest, "Thank you, sir" in return. The contagious nature of the attitude of gratitude will surprise you. Thank you for listening.

AN IMPERFECT WORLD

Ours is an imperfect world primarily because it is made up of imperfect people. During our lifetime, we shall never reach the utopia of which men dream. On this side of the Divine, there is no such thing as human perfection.

It follows, therefore, that there is no such thing as a perfect religious fellowship. If there were a perfect church, I am afraid I wouldn't be admitted into the fellowship, sinner that I am.

I once heard of a man, who when shopping around for a perfect church, heard the minister lead the congregation in the ritual, "We have done those things which we ought not to have done and have left undone those things we ought to have done." He dropped into a pew with a sign of relief, muttering, "Thank goodness I've found my crowd at last."

Which reminds me of a minister who said he was resigning from his church because of severe illness—the people were sick of him and he of them.

Although there are more than 250 nations on Earth, there are no perfect places to live. While millions of people have come here for the precious freedom to live according to the dictates of their conscience, our nation is far from perfection.

Crime is rampant. Our courts and jails are hopelessly overcrowded. We are being told that it is safer to walk the streets at night in Russia than in the United States. Is our nation coming loose at the seams? It seems so.

There are few, if any, perfect marriages. Almost half of them end in the divorce courts. A little girl asked her chum in school how she liked her new father. "Fine," said Susie. "That's odd," said Becky, "we had him last year and didn't like him at all."

When a reporter asked a couple, married for many years, if they had ever considered divorce, the wife answered thoughtfully, "Well, sometimes I have thought of choking him to death, but divorce, never."

The people in the United States are in trouble. Ours is a topsy-turvy world and, despite the fact that ours is a nation, under God, we seem to have deserted Him.

So we must, as Edna St. Vincent Millay has said, "split the sky in two, and let the face of God shine through."

That face is still there, but it is we who must look for it.

BORED WITH RELIGION?

Among nations of the world, we in America have the reputation of being a Christian nation. Yet less than one person out of five finds himself or herself in a worship service each week.

One of our distinguished university professors has made an

educated guess that people are bored with religion. Why?

It seems that one of the reasons for a cooling off process among the churches is the lack of anything sensational happening in our houses of worship. Yet we are living in the most sensational period in history.

The daily newspapers and the TV commentators are reminding us of world shaking events that are happening everywhere. The leaders of most nations are disturbed. It is almost impossible to ascertain the way the world will turn.

The very existence of hosts of people in the troubled spots of the world is at stake. Millions of people are starving to death. Other millions are on the move, looking for a chance to stay alive.

What the church is saying has been heard through the centuries. Some people are simply bored with religion.

An obvious reason for the lack of interest in religion is preoccupation. The speed of the world about us makes for crowded calendars. There are so many things to do and so little time to do them that we are exhausted even before we do the things we must do simply to live.

And today, in almost 50 percent of the homes in America, there are two breadwinners instead of one, making the calendar even the more crowded.

There seems to be no more energy left for churchgoing.

Is Christianity on a sinking ship? The matter of life's meaning crops up no matter how men seek to ignore religion.

There is a dreadful sense of inadequacy when men try to live without God. It is not the preachers, no matter their persuasiveness, who keep the church alive. It is the presence of the living God who has always been and ever shall be in His Creation who keeps the fountain of faith flowing.

As St. Augustine said, "We were made for God and find no eternal rest without Him."

FIVE GRAINS OF CORN

When the people of Colonial New England sat down to eat their Thanksgiving dinner, it was their custom to place five grains of corn beside each plate. Behind that custom is a great story.

When the 107 passengers stepped off the Mayflower on a cold November day in 1620, most of them would have starved to death had it not been for a few bushels of corn some Indians had hidden in a cave. At one time the Pilgrims were rationed only five grains a day. So in appreciation of the sacrifice of their ancestors, New Englanders for many years followed the custom of placing the corn beside the Thanksgiving plate to remind them of that dreadful first winter.

Let us imagine each one of these grains represented a particular sacrifice of our American forefathers. The first grain would represent the Pilgrims themselves. They gave us the priceless heritage of religious freedom.

Some of the members of their families probably had been burned as religious heretics. They wanted to worship God according to the dictates of their individual conscience. Thus, the first amendment to the Constitution: "Congress shall make no law respecting the establishment of religion, or prohibiting the free exercise thereof."

If you are not convinced that religious freedom is a great heritage, I suggest a trip to Russia or Iran.

The second grain of corn could represent the sacrifice of our forefathers at the Continental Congress. They took their lives in their hands when they signed the Declaration of Independence. They wrote "All men are created equal, endowed by their creator with certain inalienable rights; among these are life, liberty and the pursuit of happiness."

More than half the people in the world today are denied these basic human rights. How blessed we are.

The third grain could well represent the sacrifice of our forefathers during the Civil War, where brother fought against brother. From a blood-soaked battlefield came the words: "This nation, under God, shall have a new birth of freedom."

The fourth grain might well represent the sacrifices made on our behalf in World War I. We set out to make "the world safe for democracy" and we are still working on it.

The fifth grain could represent sacrifices made in the wars since the rise of Adolph Hitler. Through these dreadful sacrifices we are slowly learning the lessons long ago written in an ancient tomb of the Hebrew people: "Righteousness exalteth a nation but sin is a reproach to many people."

WHO ARE YOU?

Some time ago a shell-shocked soldier was attending an American Legion convention. During a pause in the program the amnesia victim jumped on the platform and cried, "Anybody here know who I am?" Luckily someone identified him and restored him to his family.

Who are you? What do you think of yourself? It is said that a man never is exactly what he thinks he is. But what he thinks, he is. What you think of yourself is tremendously important.

Consider man from the standpoint of the materialist. Twenty-three centuries ago a man by the name of Philemon wrote: "Does man differ from other animals? Only in posture. The rest are bent, but he is a wild beast who walks upright."

Two hundred years ago Lord Byron, the English poet, wrote:
"O man, thou feeble tenant of an hour,
Debased by slavery or corrupt by power;
Who knows thee well must quit thee in disgust,
Degraded mass of animated dust."

The materialistic concept of man is the essential philosophy of the Communists. They insist that all acts of men are motivated by dialectical materialism. Man makes no moral or "spiritual" decisions . . . only material. The ethical standards of the Communists are set by the leaders of the party and may vary according to the whims of the leaders.

Consider the concept of man through sacred literature. "Now ye are sons of God," writes John in the New Testament. If we think of ourselves as being the sons of the Eternal God it inevitably has a dynamic effect upon our lives.

Man is the only creature on God's earth who is created in God's image, in the spiritual likeness of God himself. For this reason he has the capacity to say these four significant words: I am, I can, I ought and I will.

I am. I am a creature designed by the creative forces of the universe. I call those creative forces God. I have been placed here for a Divine purpose.

I can. I have the capacity to fulfill the purpose for which God created me. I am not a victim of my environment. I can respond to and effect changes in my environment.

I ought. I, as a human being, have a built-in awareness of right and wrong. Men call it conscience. Alligators don't have it. Normal people do.

I will. Man is unique among the creatures of the earth in that he has freedom of will. To all intents and purposes, bullfrogs are very much alike. But there is a vast difference between men. What we are is determined by the choices we make.

No man is insignificant who has the ability to say: I am, I can, I ought, and I will.

CONSIDER THE TURTLE

It is said that when James B. Conant was president of Harvard University he kept on his desk a small toy turtle. Underneath the turtle was this inscription: "Consider the turtle. He makes progress only when he sticks out his neck."

From the standpoint of history, sticking out one's neck is old hat. It has been going on from the beginning of time. The disciples of Jesus stuck out their necks on His behalf and ten of the eleven faithful ones got their heads chopped off. The apostle Paul, writer of two-thirds of the New Testament, didn't live long enough to enjoy a Social Security check.

In all generations there have been human turtles who were courageous enough to stick out their necks in behalf of progress. Do you remember Telemacus, the diminutive monk of Rome in the third century of the Christian era? He was so disgusted with the emperor's gladiatorial combats where slaves fought to their death that he stood before the royal box and shouted: "This bloody business must stop!"

Guards cut him down in his tracks but before his blood had stained the soil on which he stood a revulsion swept over the audience and soon the combats were outlawed.

Martin Luther stuck out his neck when he nailed the Ninety-five Theses to the door of the Wittenburg church in Germany. It happened four and a half centuries ago but it started a reform movement from which all Christendom will never recover. As you might expect, Luther's retirement days were far from rosy.

Every forward thrust toward a more civilized, more humane society has been due to the willingness of someone to stick out his neck. Louis Pasteur was ridiculed and called a fool when he announced that communicable diseases were the result of invisible disease germs.

Robert Fulton's first steamship on the Hudson River was called "Fulton's Folly" but Fulton proved that fire and water could release energy hitherto unknown.

If one is bored with life, I can suggest a number of areas in which a man can stick out his neck and make a real contribution to the forward thrust of history. In the field of better racial relations, for instance. Or in the field of juvenile delinquency; or in the field of rehabilitation of the criminal; or more humane treatment of the mentally incompetent; or in the field of world peace.

Who knows but that our greatest need is for people willing to stick out their necks for causes which are of greater worth than life itself. The only trouble is you might not live long enough to enjoy it. The Carpenter of Nazareth didn't.

GANDHI: ON CHRIST'S PLAN

Since I have traveled across India several times in my life, I was eager to see the Richard Attenborough film about Mahatma Gandhi, who was portrayed by actor Ben Kingsley. During the three hours I spent in the theatre, I felt that I was in the presence of Gandhi himself.

Kingsley, half Indian, fitted the role so perfectly that I could hardly imagine the same actor could play the part of a young graduate from a British University at age twenty-five and look the part of the revered old man by the end of the film.

For many months before the film was released, Kingsley lived as Gandhi had lived—his loin cloth around his waist, his working of the spinning wheel. Kingsley beautifully presented Gandhi as he had lived.

Gandhi was a devoted Hindu, but he understood as well Jesus's philosophy of nonretaliation, turning the other cheek, going the second mile. . . . The British who controlled India were ruthless in their attempt to deal with the miserable, impoverished and unarmed Indians.

Under Gandhi's directions, the Indians, when they were clubbed or fired upon, did not retaliate.

Gandhi insisted that it would be utterly useless to meet violence with violence. He detested the religious differences that caused conflict. When confronted with an anti-Moslem crowd of Hindus, Gandhi spoke with fervor: "I am a Moslem . . . and a Hindu . . . and a Christian . . . and a Jew . . . and for God's sake, let us embrace one another like brothers." When someone referred to the British as devils, Gandhi replied, "The only devils in the world are those running around in our hearts, and that is where our battles ought to be fought."

Gandhi remained a Hindu all his life. But the bedrock of his faith was exemplified in his refusal to strike back violently. He remembered that Jesus, while on the cross, prayed for those who spat in his face.

Do you suppose that little 120-pound Hindu has given us a more accurate picture of the Man of Galilee than some among us who insist that we must strike first lest we lose the battle? We give thanks to God for that humble saint who demonstrated the power of the gospel of love in a world where hate seems to control the destiny of mankind.

KEEP YOUR SENSE OF HUMOR

Somewhere around the region of your elbow is the funny bone. If you want to locate it, try cracking your elbow on a table a time or two. It is one part of the anatomy you ought to keep well oiled and in good working order.

It might be a good idea to add one more beatitude to that wonderful list of Blesseds found in the Book of Matthew: Blessed is the man with a great sense of humor for humor hath wonderful redemptive value.

Happy is the man who can laugh at himself. Some people take themselves so seriously that they become simply a bundle of nerves, usually wind up with a nervous breakdown. They seem to carry the whole world on their backs. They can't even get a decent night's sleep because of tension and anxiety. A friend of mine says he works hard all day and then at night goes to sleep and lets God take over the night shift. Sit down some time before a mirror and, if you take yourself too seriously, take a good look at yourself. If you have any sense of humor left this ought to make you laugh.

Happy is the man who can laugh at his troubles. I have a friend who had a serious accident and suffered the loss of his right leg. I went to see him, hopefully to cheer him up. But I was in for a real surprise . . . he cheered me up! Throwing the cover back and waving the bandaged stump in my face he said, "This is a sure cure for athlete's foot."

Happy is the man who can laugh with, not at, other people. Many a tense situation at a public meeting has been dispelled because the chairman had the ability to cause the people to laugh at the proper time. You can be sure of this—people will always crowd around the person who has a good sense of humor. The sourpuss usually walks a lonesome road.

I am convinced that Jesus had a great sense of humor. He was not only a man of sorrows and acquainted with grief; he was a man of joy and acquainted with humor. He talked about the Pharisees straining gnats and swallowing camels. One can imagine a strict legalist drinking tea in the afternoon when a tiny gnat dive bombs into the hot liquid. It causes him to go through all kinds of purification ceremonies while all the time he shuts his eyes to a greater sin and swallows a camel, humps and all. The people who heard him must have roared with laughter.

Edna Wheeler Wilcox summed it up for us:

> Laugh and the world laughs with you;
> Weep, and you weep alone;
> For the sad old earth must
> borrow its mirth,
> But has trouble enough of its own.

WHY THE CHURCH?

In the Canterbury Cathedral, where the Primate of the Anglican Church is the minister, are these words of greeting: "Friend you have come to this church; leave it not without a prayer. No man entering a house ignores him who dwells in it. This is the house of God and He is here. Pray to Him who loves you and awaits your greeting. Give thanks for those who in past ages built this place and have preserved for us our heritage. Praise God for His gifts of beauty and architecture, handicraft and music. Ask that we who now live may build the spiritual fabric of the nation in truth, beauty and goodness and draw nearer to one another in perfect brotherhood. The Lord preserve thy going and thy coming in."

I believe in the church universal, Catholic, Protestant and Jewish. I have deep respect for all who seek to do God's will in the mosques and temples of worship throughout the world. There are different faces, different voices and different beliefs of the people, but there is but one God and one creator of life.

Despite the fact that many religious groups have not been faithful to their tasks, have gone off into side issues, and have been guilty of wrong actions, I still have faith in God's people and revere all houses of worship where His name is above every name.

Periodically, I set down my reasons for being a member of the church. I belong to the church because I ought to be better than I am. The church is not a gallery for the exhibition of perfect Christians, but a school for the education of imperfect ones.

I belong to the church because I want to pay my debts and do my share toward discharging my obligation to society. I want to be as fair to my children as my parents were fair to me. I belong to the church because of the memories of the things I can never forget, the faces that will never fade, and the vows I have resolved to keep as long as life lasts.

I belong to the church because of the strong persons in it who reinforce me, and the weak men who need my encouragement. I belong to the church because of the hope I have for the world of tomorrow and the responsibility I have of helping God build His kind of world with peace, goodwill and social justice for all mankind.

SLEEPING THROUGH THE STORM

Years ago, in a typical English village, it was the custom of men who were seeking employment to come to the town square on

Monday morning. If someone wanted his house painted, his crops harvested or his livestock cared for, he would come to the square and pick his man.

One morning a farmer came looking for a farm hand to help him in his work. He questioned a robust young fellow about his farm experience to discern whether or not he could qualify for the job. But to every question the farmer asked, the young man replied with an unusual answer: "I can always sleep on a stormy night."

This seemed a peculiar answer but the farmer took a chance and put the young man to work.

Some weeks later a flash storm struck in the dead of night. The rains came in torrents and the winds blew with cyclonic force. Fearing for the safety of his stock, the farmer rushed to the room of his helper to awaken him. But the sole response to the heavy knocks on the door was the rhythmic snoring of the sleeper.

Rushing out to see about things for himself, to his utter surprise, he found everything in order despite the storm. The livestock, showing no evidence of stampeding, were securely fastened in their stalls. Even the chickens were not unusually perturbed. There were no doors slamming, no pieces of tin on the barn roof flapping in the wind, no hayricks being blown away.

When the farmer returned to bed he remembered the words of the workman the day he was employed: "I can always sleep on a stormy night." He had done his work so well that, when the storm came, he had no cause for worry.

Storms are inevitable. There is the storm of physical testing. One's ability to pass through the physical crisis may largely be determined by the preparation one makes before the crisis comes.

There is the storm of financial reversal. But the adequacy of one's foresight largely determines one's ability to ride out the financial crisis involving the family.

There is the storm of mental testing. When the chips are down the reward for the promotion to the position of larger responsibility usually goes to the person who has not waited for the final examination to get the facts.

There is the storm of temptation of one's best self. He is best able to weather this storm if, through the years, he has committed himself to fixed habits of worthy living. Given these situations, one can learn to appreciate the young man's answer to the questions asked: "I can always sleep on a stormy night."

WHO GOES THERE?

A sentry was walking his beat between two armies poised to strike in the dead of night. He heard a faint footstep in the black darkness before him. Should he ask, "Who goes there?" What would the answer be? A bullet? The voice of a brother? Or absolute silence? Millions of people have had this experience as they stood out under the stars, probably alone, in the darkness of the night, and have cried to the heavens, "Is anybody there? Where are you, God?"

Some have come back with a wistful agnosticism. The heavens were splashed with a big question mark. Some come back with bitter atheism. Nobody there . . . pitifully weak souls in a vast universe utterly alone. Others came back with the deep assurance of the writer of the first book in the Bible, "In the beginning, God . . ."

While there is obviously only one God, He is known by many names. Aristotle talked about "The Unmoved Mover." Spencer said "Eternal Energy." Huxley made reference to "The Unknown Absolute." Others have used such phrases as "First Principle," "Process of Integration," "Supreme Intelligence"—all the way down to "The Big Boss" or the "Man Upstairs."

But Jesus called Him Father! Not some mechanical mind, some all-powerful force like electricity. Jesus did not teach us to pray, "Cosmic Essence, hallowed be thy name." But Father, indicative of personhood. Jesus said, "If you know how to give good gifts unto your children, how much more shall your heavenly Father give . . ."

When Jesus called God Father He evidently assumed that God had limited Himself by His fatherhood. No father is almighty in that he can do anything. A father must wait for his child to grow up, to learn . . . a father is limited by his fatherhood. So God limits Himself. He doesn't make planes that cannot crash, or, having given men freedom, create human beings that cannot sin.

Jesus called God Father because a father is one who seeks His children. Is history man's long quest for God? It could be that it is the other way around. Are we knocking on His door or is He knocking on ours? God is not hidden. John writes, "Behold, I stand at the door and knock. He is out there on that long, toilsome road—calling our names.

'DESIDERATA' OFFERS GOOD ADVICE

Many years ago, historians found an old plaque called "Desiderata" in St. Paul's Church in Baltimore, Maryland, dated 1692. Despite the passage of the years, its truths remain priceless. It has good Independence Day advice.

"Go placidly amid the noise and haste and remember what peace there may be in silence. As far as possible without surrender, be on good terms with all persons. Speak your truth quietly and clearly. Listen to others, even the dull and ignorant. They, too, have their story. If you compare yourself with others, you may become vain and bitter. There will always be greater and lesser persons than yourself.

"Keep interested in your own career, however humble. It is a real possession in the changing fortune of time. Exercise caution in your business affairs. The world is full of trickery. But let not this blind you to what virtue there is. Everywhere life is full of heroism.

"Be yourself. Do not feign affection. Neither be cynical about love, for in the face of all aridity and disenchantment it is as perennial as the grass. Take kindly the counsel of the years, gracefully surrendering the things of youth. Nurture strength of spirit to shield you in sudden misfortune. Do not distress yourself with imaginings. Many fears are born of fatigue and loneliness. Beyond a wholesome discipline, be gentle with yourself.

"You are a child of the universe, no less than the trees and the stars. You have a right to be here. And whether or not it is clear to you, no doubt the universe is unfolding as it should. Therefore be at peace with God, whatever you conceive Him to be. Whatever your labors and aspirations in the noisy confusion of life, keep peace with your soul. With all its shame, drudgery and broken dreams, it is still a beautiful world. Be careful and strive to be happy."

IT'S IN THE BOOK

At last I found it. I knew all the time it ought to be in the Bible. And there it was in the fourteenth verse of the second chapter of Paul's letter to the Philippians. It reads: "Do all things without grumbling."

If there is anyone who really gets under my skin it is the fellow who, regardless of the most favorable circumstances, always comes up with something to grumble about.

I once knew a man whose sullen face indicated that he drank a quart of green persimmon juice for breakfast each morning. There was literally nothing his family could do that would please him.

When his patient wife asked him how he wanted his eggs cooked, he gruffly replied that he wanted one of them fried and the other scrambled. When she brought them to the table he shoved them aside, saying "You scrambled the wrong egg."

Some people are born in the objective case. They never seem satisfied unless they are grumbling about something or someone. They don't get along with the members of their own family, with the neighbors, with the people with whom they work, with the city fathers, with the politicans, all the way up to the president and U.S. Congress.

I believe the friends of Jesus who grumble about everything on earth do more harm for the cause of Christianity than his bitter enemies. Their type of religion is about as attractive as the seven-year itch.

A minister once asked a grumbling, sour-faced parishioner if she were happy. "Yes I am," she said. He replied, "Then, please notify your face."

PROPERTY CAME FIRST

Sometime ago I read a newspaper account of a public auction held in the year 1825. Among the many items to be auctioned off, these two items, linked together, impressed me very much: "A five-year old dark bay trotting horse; and Sarah, a twenty-year-old Negro girl, general housework, valued at $900 and guaranteed." "A bay horse—and Sarah" I kept muttering to myself. "A bay horse and Sarah."

This leads me to say that the capital crime of recorded history is incarnated in this one phrase. We continue to put property before people. That is what caused the French Revolution—putting the property of royalty before the hunger of the masses of people. "Let them eat cake" the queen said. That is what is behind the economic revolution going on in the world today—putting property rights before the rights of economically disenfranchised people. "A bay horse and Sarah" is history repeating itself. The words are different but the problem is the same.

Authentic Christianity deals with the three fundamental hungers of the human spirit. The primary hunger is for bread. Man cannot live by bread alone but he cannot live long without it. Our basic problem is not simply the impoverishment of the earth. With our technical knowledge, the earth can possibly sustain all people in physical comfort. But the impoverishment of the heart . . . that's our basic problem. Distributors of bread must remember that all people are people "for whom Christ died." The problem is not simply the crust of bread (made of flour) but willingness to be brotherly (made of love).

The second fundamental hunger of man is for knowledge. It is the responsibility of the people who are enlightened to share their knowledge with those who sit in darkness. Unless we share the truth with those in darkness, their darkness will destroy us. Ignorant people are among those "for whom Christ died."

The third basic hunger of the human heart is for love . . . the desire to be appreciated. No civilization can long endure without recognition of the principle of human dignity. I have never known anyone who really wanted to be a second class citizen. The unloved masses of the world are those "for whom Christ died." Long ago, one of God's prophets stated it like this: "For God so loved the world . . ." not the ground under our feet but the people in our midst.

THE WORD IS INTEGRITY

There is an interesting story about one of our heroes in the Korean war, General Dean, a captive of the Communist forces. He was captured in the little town of Chong-ju and was told by the enemy that he would be given thirty minutes in which to write a farewell note to his family. He was morally certain that in the course of the day he would be taken out, placed against a wall and shot.

What do you suppose was in the letter which General Dean imagined would be his last word to his family? It consisted of only eight or ten lines, but right down in the middle of it General Dean said, "Tell Bill the word is integrity." This was the advice of a heroic father to his teenage son.

I would like for you to have that word stick in your mind like a burr. General Dean could have said the word is security, or happiness or popularity. Most fathers wish for their sons all of these things. But the general chose the word integrity. Integrity means character, honesty, wholeness. It is a quality of character desperately needed in every generation, particularly our own. Honesty is the bedrock on which we build an enduring civilization.

The quality of honesty has been revered throughout human history. One of the ancient commandments Moses brought down from atop Sinai was, "Thou shalt not bear false witness." The Book of Proverbs says, "He who tells the truth is in the majority even if he stands alone." Alfred Tennyson, Englishman of letters, said of the Duke of Wellington, hero of the battle of Waterloo, "He never sold the truth to serve the hour."

In the complex age in which we live we have dozens of ways of lying to each other. We can lie by exaggeration. A frightened boy said to his mother that he saw a big black bear in his bedroom. The mother investigated, found the story a fabrication and insisted that her son ask God for forgiveness for telling a story. When she asked if God had forgiven him he said, "Yes, God thought it was a bear too, when He first saw it." We have to constantly remind ourselves that all of the things said in the advertisements simply are highly exaggerated. It is unfortunate that hosts of government agencies have to be always on the alert to preserve some modicum of truth in advertising.

We can lie by insinuation. We can lie by telling half-truths. We can lie by pasting labels on people. This is the most popular form of lying at the moment, particularly in an election year. When someone makes the blanket statement that this or that person is un-American, a pinko, a comsimp, a Neanderthal conservative, an arch radical, you may be sure that person is not telling the whole truth. After all, who knows the whole truth about anyone?

Both presidential candidates have been saying something about "Come home America" meaning of course, come home to their side. I, too, would wish America to come home to her apparently lost idealism. Come home America . . . to honesty, to integrity, to God. Come home to that quality of character found in honest Abe Lincoln who, when leaving Springfield for Washington as President said, "I go to Washington not knowing when or if ever I shall return. With God's help I cannot fail. Without it I cannot succeed."

LINCOLN: A MAN OF FAITH

Abraham Lincoln who, as we remember from our school days, became the sixteenth president of the United States. In all the pages of American history, probably no other man has been more maligned . . . or more beloved—maligned during his lifetime, beloved after his assassination.

Lincoln was born in a log cabin near Hodgenville, Kentucky, in 1809. He was almost totally deprived of a formal education, having spent less than a year in a school room by the time he was eighteen years old. Lincoln, however, was determined to educate himself. He would walk miles to borrow what few books his friends had to lend him.

He became a lawyer by simply devouring the law books at his disposal. He ran for Congress, won a first term but was defeated for a second. He sought appointment as Commissioner of the General Land Office but did not receive it. He ran for the U.S. Senate and lost. But his famous Lincoln-Douglas debates over slavery made him a national figure.

He was elected president in 1860 and again in 1864, but John Wilkes Booth's assassination took him from us forty days after the second inaugural. Almost immediately after Lincoln's inauguration the Civil War began. It was one of the most devastating wars in history as members of households fought against each other.

Mr. Lincoln had his enemies in both camps. He was slandered, maligned, called the original gorilla, an atheist, an infidel. While he belonged to no church, he frequently attended the New York Avenue Presbyterian Church when he was president. But he loved people! He consistently defended his anti-slavery stand. He was a man of great sympathy.

No one knows how many homesick boys of the Union Army who went AWOL were spared heavy sentences because of a sympathetic president. When Mrs. Bixby of Boston lost her five sons in battle, Lincoln wrote her saying, "I pray that our Father might assuage the anguish of your bereavement."

When he proudly signed the Emancipation Proclamation he said, "I know there is a God and that he hates prejudice and slavery. He has a work for me to do and I am ready. I am nothing, but truth is everything. I know I am right for Christ teaches it."

In his Gettysburg Address he said, "This nation, under God, shall have a new birth of freedom and the government of the people, by the people and for the people shall not perish from the earth." Surely this man had a magnificent faith.

As has been said, Lincoln was one of the most denounced . . . and the most dedicated of all our presidents. Let me recount the words of Ralph Waldo Emerson, who said we must judge history not by the days or the years but against the backdrop of the centuries. Public opinion is as variable as the wind. After all, public opinion idolized Marilyn Monroe and crucified Jesus Christ.

WE LIVE IN DEEDS, NOT DAYS

All you have to do to get your name in the paper is to grab a firm hold on life and live to be a hundred years old. If you have never seen your name in print, have never seen your picture in the local gossip sheet, make the announcement that you are soon to have your hundredth birthday and someone will be around for a story. An old man up in the Arkansas Ozarks came to this magic hundredth birthday and told the reporter the key to his longevity. He said he never smoked, never drank, never used coffee or tea, never caroused, never played golf, never argued with his wife, always went to bed at eight o'clock in the evening. Why he wanted to live to be a hundred years old I'll never know.

As far as I know, the man who has the record for longevity was a man mentioned in the Bible by the name of Methuselah. The book of Genesis says that he lived to be 969 years old. I do not like to speak disparagingly of the dead because they cannot defend themselves. Nevertheless I have some difficulty in having great respect for the old fellow. If in all that time Methuselah ever did anything worthwhile, no one got around to mentioning it. His complete biography is crowded into one sentence: "And the days of Methuselah were 969 years, and he died." After nine and two-thirds centuries that is about all a man could do isn't it . . . just haul off and die. It seems after all those years of living he didn't even die a natural death. He must have accidentally drowned. He was in fact Noah's grandfather and when Noah got all those pairs of living things in the ark he may have just let the old man drown.

In these days when food is rather expensive I get to wondering just how much food Methuselah ate in his lifetime. It must have been several train loads. If he went to as many church suppers as I have gone to, I wonder how much meat loaf he ate. Someone told me that if all the meat loaf he had eaten were laid end to end . . . he would let it lie there. And I can understand that! I wonder how many pairs of pants Methuselah wore out. And if he sat around the Courthouse whittling all that time I have a pretty good idea of where he wore them out. If they had had Social Security in those days he would have bankrupted the government. Imagine drawing a government check the third of every month for 904 years.

In sharp contrast to this long life of apparent uselessness, consider the life of Jesus, thirty-three years in length. The libraries of the world are filled with stories of the influence of this matchless man of Galilee. He split the calendar into B.C. and A.D. and put church spires all over the world. The poet had it right. We live in deeds, not days. It is not how long we live that matters. It is what we live for.

ON SEGREGATING GOD

One of our contemporary philosophers has written: "We have gotten rid of God, not by denying him but by reducing him to a nonentity."

Obviously this is not a true statement. It is absurd to imagine that a creation can dethrone its creator. Denial of the reality of God is simply one man's opinion, not God's destruction.

However, this philosopher has called our attention to a serious problem in our day. We have literally tried to reduce God to nothing more than a three-letter word. The thesis of some people is that while God may be real, he is irrelevant.

We call on him and we get no direct answer. We have problems and he doesn't seem to be of any help whatever. We call him the man upstairs and he seems to be too busy to come down the stairs where we live. So we actually dismiss God by putting him in a corner. We segregate him from the daily routine of living.

We segregate God when we divide time into God's time and man's time. We remember to keep the sabbath day holy. But what about the other six days? We cannot possibly keep one day holy if we spend the other six days without regard for the sanctity of life itself. To put God in one segment of time only is but to deny God who is the father of all time.

We segregate God when we falsely separate biblical truth from scientific truth. The Bible contains all the truth that is essential for personal and world redemption. But surely no one believes that all of God's truth is contained within those pages.

And if I get snake bitten, I am going to take the doctor's advice even if I don't find such action prescribed in the Bible. Since God has always been communicating with men, I am willing to assume he speaks to surgeons, scientists, astronomers and whoever else will listen.

We segregate God when we attempt to separate God's work from man's work. God put the first pair, Adam and Eve, in a garden. He evidently meant for them to work their garden.

Jesus himself was a carpenter, made a living for his widowed mother and his younger brothers and sisters. Is not all honorable work God's work?

We deceive ourselves when we segregate God from the mainstream of life. In such futile attempts we only segregate ourselves from God.

GREAT EVENTS TURN ON SMALL HINGES

Some years ago I visited Damascus, capital city of Syria. My guide took me to the wall where, in New Testament times, the Apostle Paul escaped from his enemies.

His life had been threatened and his friends hoisted him on top of a fifteen-foot wall and lowered him by ropes in a basket. (Acts 9:23). What if the rope had broken and Paul had been killed? It would have changed the course of history because more than half of the New Testament was written by Paul. Great events turn on small hinges.

Three thousand years ago King Pharaoh held the Hebrews in his dominion in abject slavery. In order to keep the Hebrew population under control, he ordered all male babies destroyed. One Hebrew mother kept her infant son a secret for several weeks. When she could no longer hide him, she made a little boat for him and hopefully set him afloat on the Nile river.

When Pharaoh's daughter came down for her afternoon swim she saw the little baby, fell in love with him, took him home with her and reared him as her own son.

His name was Moses, leader of his people out of Egyptian bondage and spiritual father of the Hebrew nation. Great events turn on small hinges. What if Pharaoh's daughter had neglected to take a swim that day?

In the year A.D. 732 at the battle of Tours, Christian Charles Martel defeated the leader of the Moslem forces, and western Europe and the Americas reaped a Christian culture. I make no judgment here but simply say great events turn on small hinges.

In the year 1870 in Russia a little boy by the name of Nicolai Lenin was born. When seventeen years of age, his older brother Alexander was hanged for taking part in a plot against the Czar. From that moment, young Lenin became a revolutionary and is largely responsible for the Communist philosophy, now embraced by a third of the people of the earth.

When Adolph Hitler was a teenager he attended a Protestant Sunday School. He resented all talk about equality and grew up literally hating all people of Jewish blood. He precipitated the World War II and was largely responsible for the death of millions of people and the destruction of billions of dollars worth of property.

Great events in our own lives turn on small hinges. Impulsive decisions often call for decades of remorse. In a thinly populated area of northern Canada there was once a sign at the fork of a road which read, "Be careful which road you take; you will be in it for hundreds of miles."

DOES GOD GUIDE?

One of the ships in the Marine Museum of Oslo, Norway, is called the Fram. It was the ship used by the Norwegian explorer Fridtjof Nansen when he visited the North Pole during the early years of this century. It was sailed as far north as it could go, was finally frozen amid the icebergs. Then the explorers took their dog sleds and began the overland journey. When they pushed as far north as possible with their heavy equipment, Nansen tells how they built an igloo of ice and installed their little oil burning stove. They waited for the winds to die down and the weather to clear to make the last dash to victory. But the weather would not cooperate and the delay was longer than expected. Then their precious fuel ran low and they became fearful of death. Furthermore, they had no contact with the outside world.

Nansen took a little carrier pigeon out of its cage, pitched it into the 70 degree below zero wind, hoping it would find its way to its Oslo home where Mrs. Nansen was anxiously awaiting word from her husband. Disappearing amid the swirling clouds of snow, the pigeon some time later dropped down on the very window sill where Mrs. Nansen was waiting. She read the two numbers on the band around the foot of the pigeon indicating the party's location and soon a rescue party brought the intrepid explorers back home.

When I hear people question God's ability to guide them in their daily tasks, I think of this story. How did the little pigeon know where home was? Did God put a divine antenna in a pigeon's brain? If God can guide a pigeon through the frozen northland to its roost, surely He can put His hand on my shoulder and tell me "That's right" and "That's wrong." As I see it, no man is lost who knows the way home.

FAITH CAN HUMBLE THE MOST WORLDLY

About forty years ago, two missionaries, a husband and wife team, went to the Belgian Congo, now called Zaire, and established a missionary outpost in the heart of the jungle.

They were the proud parents of an exceptionally talented daughter, who, according to reports, had a magnificent singing voice. The parents were determined to give their daughter as good a musical education as possible in the United States.

They sent her to Chicago, where she was admitted at one of the universities in the city. Fortunately, she found a part time job singing in a nightclub, for which she was paid $150 a week. That amount of money was quite large for a singer in her teens.

The club was owned by Al Brown, a well-to-do person who lived in the tenderloin area of the metropolis. Brown was so impressed with the young singer that he insisted she visit him in his suite of rooms after working hours in his luxurious downtown hotel.

We in America have watched enough television in our day to know why she had been summoned to his room in the middle of the night. Realizing her dilemma too late, she prayed earnestly that she might be delivered from her exploiter. She explained in no uncertain terms who she was and who she hoped to be.

The next day, the teenage girl received a large bouquet of orchids, each with a $100 bill in the center. The note said: "The flowers are for you. The bills are for your parents."

As most know, Al Brown was better known as Al Capone, at one time the most powerful underworld character in U.S. history. At least once in his lifetime, Capone responded to the fervent prayers of a teenage girl who had anchored her faith in the visible presence of the living Christ.

President Abraham Lincoln once said: "I have been driven to my knees so many times by the overwhelming conviction that I had nowhere else to go."

And so have we all.

WE WORSHIP MANY GODS

It is simply not true that all men are either theists, atheists or agnostics. It is more realistic to say that all men are polytheists, worshipers of many gods.

Throughout history we find a constant stream of gods making their debut, being worshiped, then sinking into oblivion. Tacitus, historian of the first century after Christ said that there were more gods in Rome than there were men. Some of the more famous ones were Bacchus, god of revelry; Mars, god of war; Minerva, goddess of wisdom; Mercury, god of commerce; Apollo and Venus, god and goddess of beauty. Even the heavenly bodies were worshiped as gods. There was a sun god from whence we get the name Sunday; a moon god from whence comes Monday; a thunder god called Thor from whence the name Thursday; Saturn the god of the harvest from whence the name Saturday.

From the standpoint of theology, it is true that human beings are divided between the theists and the atheists. But from the standpoint of psychology every man has a god. His god is what he loves most, cares most about, that for which he will make the supreme sacrifice of his life.

Most of us believe that the real God is creator of the Universe and makes us in His image, His likenness. But there are man-made gods whose image is like that of their worshipers. We have a tendency to become like the god we worship.

Bacchus is an ancient god who still holds great power over man in our day. Bacchus is the god of revelry and drunkenness. It is estimated that ten million Americans today are virtual slaves to this god. The total cost of worshiping this god is estimated as high as $25 billion. Even this figure does not include the loss of life by accidents and the misery endured by members of the alcoholic's family.

Does anyone suppose that Apollo and Venus, god and goddess of beauty, died with the Roman Empire? It is sobering to consider the fact that more money is spent on the physical adornment of the body than on the training of the minds of the youth of our land. Do not misunderstand me. All of us could use a beauty treatment or two. But when we accentuate physical adornment we worship at Apollo's sacred shrine.

And what of the worship of Mars, god of war? To be sure we must keep up our defenses. But sometimes a few million dollars to feed the hungry would be a better investment than a few billion dollars for instruments of death. Conceivably the U.S. arsenal can stand up to any attack made upon our own soil. If this is the case, we should not be stampeded into bankruptcy by the worshipers of Mars who would rely solely on brute force.

At long last, life is a choice between gods. And the ultimate choice is still between the gods we make and the God who made us.

PEOPLE FENCE THEMSELVES IN

Once I visited a white leghorn-fryer farm where chickens were being fattened for table use. I found that the chickens never get to touch the ground "from hatching to axing." They are put into scientifically sterilized feeders where they stand until they are ready to be eaten.

How could a chicken be happy under such circumstances? No chance to dig in the ground and uncover a nice, juicy worm; not a chance to roam in the garden and pick the bugs off the lettuce.

When I go to the zoo I notice that the tigers, leopards and hyenas, pacing up and down in their cages, always seem to be mad. I feel sorry for them because they are always fenced in. Of course, I would feel sorry for myself if there were no fence between us.

Look at some of the fences people build around themselves. With high-pressure salesmanship and "no money down" payments, many people with stated incomes succumb to the temptation of buying things for which they cannot pay. They pin themselves down with obligations, and any little family emergency throws them into a fit. The seriousness of this situation becomes obvious when we realize that many marriages have been dissolved because of a too extravagant wife or husband—or both.

I have known men who have fenced themselves in because of a blind devotion to ambition. They have set for themselves certain financial or social goals and, when they were not attained on schedule, they became frustrated and went to pieces. This is no argument against having a worthy ambition. It is a warning against the worship of what we sometimes erroneously call success.

And what of the people who have fenced themselves in because of their own pride and prejudices? As a Protestant, I am richer because I have a great Jewish friend, a wonderful Catholic friend. As a white Anglo-Saxon American, I am richer because my circle of friends includes black Americans, Latin-Americans, Japanese-Americans, Chinese-Americans. I want to remember that I am richer because I am a part of a neighborhood that includes 220 million people. After all, there is but one race—the human race.

Edwin Markham spoke to our needs when he wrote:
He drew a circle that shut me out—
Heretic, rebel, a thing to flout.
But Love and I had the wit to win:
We drew a circle that took him in.

THROW YOUR CRUTCHES AWAY

Back in the good old days of barbershop quartets, one of the favorite songs was "Hand Me Down My Walking Cane." With genuine respect and deep appreciation for all who are forced to use crutches for ambulatory purposes, I would like to write a song titled "Hang Up Your Walking Cane."

We have hosts of people who are running around with "crutches" to support them when they ought to be traveling under their own steam. In John 5 of the New Testament there is an account of a lame man who had been lying near the pool of Bethesda for thirty-eight years waiting for someone to help him get into the water, which had curative powers. Jesus asked him, "Do you want to be healed?"

"Of course," the man said.

Then Jesus said, "Rise, take up your pallet and walk."

I suppose no one really knows if this was a psychological or a physiological healing. In any case, Jesus seemed to have said, "Your trouble is not only in your bones but in your brains. You labor under the assumption that you cannot get along without a cane. Throw your crutches away."

I talked to a person some time ago who used a "cane" to support his sagging mental frame when he should have been standing on his own feet. His excuse, or crutch, was his lack of a college education when he was growing up.

Obviously, no man in his right mind would argue against the importance of a formal education. But I have met brilliant people who never set foot in college and dumb people who have framed degrees all over their walls. The person who is willing to use a little brain, sweat and muscle can make a success of something no matter the educational handicap. He is wise to throw that crutch away.

There are thousands of people who say, "I am a victim of bad luck. I was born under an unlucky star." We all admit that some people are lucky, some unlucky. But it occurs to me that often the people who work the hardest and use their brains the most are the people to whom good luck seems to come. The circumstances of birth have little to do with a person's worth. We are better off if we throw that "cane" away.

Other people say, "My problem is heredity. My weaknesses are the result of the failures of my parents . . . arguments . . . separation . . . divorce." These are always a convenient crutch when we refuse to take responsibility for our own acts. But the argument will not hold up.

Generally speaking, our troubles are not because of our parents . . . but ours alone. Let's be honest . . . hang up that "cane" . . . and move out on our own two feet. How is that for a good New Year's resolution?

SOME THOUGHTS ON LONGEVITY

If you want to get your name and picture in the newspaper, all you have to do is to live to be a hundred years old.

An old man who lived up in the hills of Arkansas attributed his long life to never drinking coffee, never smoking or chewing tobacco, never attending school or church, never going to a movie, never watching TV, never arguing with his wife, and always working seven days a week. Why he even wanted to live to be a hundred years old, I will never know.

As far as history is concerned, the person who has the longest record for longevity is a man named Methuselah, who is mentioned in the Book of Genesis. "And the days of Methuselah were nine hundred and sixty-nine years; and he died." What else could a man do but die after such a long life?

I often have wondered what that benign gentleman did during that long period of time. Think of the amount of food he must have consumed. And with today's prices? If he had gone to as many church dinners as I have, how much meat loaf would he have eaten?

If all the meat loaf I have eaten were laid end to end, I think I would let it lie there. How many pairs of pants do you suppose he wore out? And if he sat around as much as we do, I have a good idea where he wore them out.

If they had had social security in those days, dear old Methuselah would have bankrupt the government. Imagine drawing a third-of-the-month check for 904 years.

There is no telling how long Methuselah would have lived if he had died a natural death. He evidently drowned in the flood. Noah was his grandson and when God told Noah to build an ark, there is no record of the grandfather getting aboard.

By way of contrast to Methuselah's long life, consider the life of Jesus—only 33 years. Yet Jesus unveiled the face of God, split the calendar into B.C. and A.D. and put spires and crosses across the skyline of the world.

The poets are right . . . we live in deeds, not days. It is not how long we live that matters so much as what we live for.

EMERGENCY RELIGION

In Shakespeare's play "The Tempest," one of the characters screams, "To prayers, to prayers, all is lost." Is prayer to be used in emergencies only? Is religion a fire-escape affair? Do we serve God simply to escape the torment of the damned?

It's obvious a person's religion actually does get him out of trouble. Breaking the laws of God means trouble and Christ came to show us God's way. Purposeless living means trouble and Christ came to help us make our lives useful.

The Bible is filled with accounts of God hearing the prayers of persons in trouble. Jonah got into trouble running away from God. He booked passage on a ship going in the wrong direction. A storm arose and the sailors said the cause of the storm was

Jonah seeking to flee from God's presence. They tossed him over-board, a big fish swallowed him and Jonah found himself in a whale of a lot of trouble.

Imagine absolute darkness, wall to wall stomach, no fresh air to breathe. So Jonah prayed, the fish delivered him and Jonah hit the land running to do God's will.

But here is a seemingly contradictory fact. Religion often gets you into trouble. During the World War II when Adolph Hitler commanded all ministers to preach hatred against the Jews, there were untold numbers of martyrs who lost their lives for con-science sake.

When Martin Luther King fought against the rules that dis-criminated against black people, he got into trouble. When Gandhi identified himself, for conscience sake, with sixty mil-lion impoverished untouchables in India, he spent much of the rest of his life in jail as a protest. Religion gets people into real trouble.

Religion also is a great insulator against trouble. The prodigal son is always welcome to the Father's house. But the son who never leaves is to be preferred. The bird with a broken pinion, it is said, never flies as high again.

TOO FEW REPORT FOR DUTY

In most of the Protestant hymnals in America there is a song titled *"Onward Christian Soldiers."* In it, there is a line which runs *"Like a mighty army moves the church of God."* I have never been in the armed services, but I have two brothers and a son who served their time when called upon to do so. Yet I have never heard any of them say the armed forces reminded them of the movement of the church in our day.

Let us suppose that the armed forces actually did move like the contemporary church today. Imagine reveille at six in the morn-ing. The sergeant barks, "Count fours!"

"One." "Two." "Three." Then silence . . . Four is missing.

"Where is Private Smith?"

A buddy pipes up, "Sergeant, Private Smith was at a dance last night, and, it being Saturday, he decided to catch up on his sleep this morning. He asked me to convey to you his good wishes and say to you that he is with you in spirit."

"Thanks, old buddy," says the sergeant. "Give Smith my love the next time you see him."

The count reaches another gap.

"Where is Private Brown?" asks the sergeant.

"I'm sorry, sir," chirps a chap. "Private Brown has a foursome at the golf links today. They tee off at 11, and since Brown works six days a week, Sunday is the only day he has for recreation and you know how important that is."

"Yes I know, I hope he has a nice game," says the sergeant.

"Where is Private Jones?" asks the sergeant.

A squeaky voice answers, "Mr. Jones asked me to tell you that he had to mow the lawn this morning, sir. Competent help is so difficult to come by that he must do it himself. It's his wife's orders."

"I can understand that, I'm married myself," says the sergeant.

"Where is Private Jackson?" yells the sergeant.

"Sir, Private Jackson asked me to tell you that he and his wife are expecting company for dinner and he has to stay home and help cook. He sends his regrets."

"Sorry I asked the questions," says the sergeant. "I hope I haven't embarrassed anyone."

If that were the way the Army moved, we would be in a bad way for defense. It would be a great day when the church really moves like a mighty army . . . for world peace, world understanding, nuclear freeze and world brotherhood.

GOD IN BUSINESS

There have been times in history when the soldier was the leading citizen. In the golden age of Greece the scholar climbed up in the driver's seat. In India, for a time, the leading citizens were among the priests. In the United States it would seem that the leading citizen is Mr. Business Man. American business men exercise tremendous power in shaping the future of our country.

This has not always been so. Merchants in general were mistrusted because they were considered unreliable. Deception was considered good business and the motto was: "Let the buyer beware." To be sure, there are still scalpers on Main Street, USA. Every day some of them are caught and turned over to government authorities for prosecution. But, by and large, the piratical days of dishonest merchandising are on the wane.

The businesses that prosper have invariably been businesses where customers bought with a sense of solid confidence. Some of the teachings of the churches have become the foundations of our better business organizations. For instance:

Modern business men turn the other cheek. Agnostics may ridicule Jesus' teaching concerning the other cheek, but big business has found it profitable to do so day after day. "The customer is always right" is the slogan of the house. Salesmen and clerks are trained to be courteous; they know that courtesy pays off. Few people can withstand the persuasiveness of friendliness and good will.

Modern business men rely upon faith. Skeptics insist that those who rely on faith will be robbed, but business men of integrity thrive on it.

By faith we eat food we do not see cooked, prepared by chefs we have never met, served by waiters we do not know.

By faith we buy milk we have not inspected, take medicine handed to us by unknown pharmacists, prescribed by doctors who are reluctant to explain everything to us.

By faith we buy certain merchandise from certain merchants because of the reputation of the firm for honesty.

By faith the merchant trusts us to pay at the end of the month just as we trust him to stand behind his goods.

Modern business men bear each other's burdens. It is not uncommon for one bank to come to the rescue of another in trouble. Insurance companies come to the rescue of other insurance companies in time of stress. Business men who are in competition with each other will work side by side to establish better codes of business ethics in the community.

The soundest businesses in our community are built on the soundest moral principles. Neither a house nor a business built on an unsound foundation can ultimately survive.

LETTER TO MADISON AVENUE ADMEN

I have never been particularly interested in writing letters to editors. They are probably as set in their ways as I am and nothing I could say would change their minds. Besides, I don't think editors read them anyway. But I cannot postpone the urge to write the Madison Avenue men who concoct those TV commercials to which I am forced to listen. Here is what I would say to them. "Dear (in a manner of speaking) Avenue: I have never written an entire avenue before but I hope someone takes this letter to your next party and reads it out loud. I have been listening to your TV commercials since I wore rompers and you must admit my powers of endurance are rather well developed. I hope you don't mind my giving you a little homey advice. I know you won't take it but you will do me a favor if you let me get it off my chest.

"First, yelling is a poor way to carry on a conversation. I often take a walk during the commercials but it does no good since I can still hear you from the refrigerator in the kitchen. Did you ever hear a man proposing to a girl over a loud speaker? Cut down the volume. We are not deaf but we will be if you keep screaming.

"Second, too much is plenty! Have you ever heard of the saturation point? That is the point at which the greatest possible amount of substance has been absorbed. I reach mine about the two-thousandth time I am told that X-brand coffee is real coffee. The century-long battle between Anacin and Excedrin gives me a headache. My stomach doesn't feel too good either.

"Third, a wisecrack loses its novelty after the first ten thousand times. When we hear the endless chain of letters like "duz duz everything" we make a chain of our own, like "fgs su" which means "for goodness sake, shut up."

"Fourth, truth in advertising would be a good advertisers' slogan. That is a good motto for politicians, preachers, business men, blue-collar workers, husbands, wives, sons, daughters, everybody. William Shakespeare said it like this: "To thine own self be true, and it must follow, as the night the day, thou canst not then be false to any man.""

HAVING FUN DOING WITHOUT

When the Yankee poet Henry David Thoreau, the recluse, made one of his infrequent journeys from Walden Pond to the nearby village store, a friend asked him what he saw. Thoreau said, "I saw a thousand things I can do without."

Most of the advertising in our day is calculated to create discontent with what we have. New model cars are coming off the assembly line annually so we will have to trade our older cars to keep up to date. Styles in clothes are constantly changing so we will buy new clothes more often than necessary. New merchandise is attractively displayed in the show windows to tempt us to say, "I just can't do without that any longer."

Sometime ago, in a California bird book, I saw advertised a blue-violet bird of some sort that whistled tunes, knows four hundred words and sells for $1,500. That is one thing I can do without. I get four hundred words every morning for breakfast—for free. As for tunes we have two radios and a TV and one of them is going all the time. I saw a Persian rug hanging in an antique shop with a price tag of $25,000 on it. If I had that much money I certainly wouldn't want to spend it for something I would be stepping on all the time. That's another item I can do without.

I think the key to contentment is not in having what you like but in liking what you have. I have learned what money cannot buy—health, friendship, a fairly sound mind, freedom; unpurchaseable things.

I've often thought of Jesus' words about laying up treasures in heaven where neither moth nor rust consumes and where thieves do not break through and steal. Jesus is saying that we ought to invest not in things that perish, but in the things that are eternal. Christian stewardship is taking the things that we cannot possibly keep (there are no pockets in shrouds) and investing them in things we cannot possibly lose (good causes, enduring friendships, the Kingdom of God).

TEN RULES FOR HUSBANDS

Since June is the month for marriages, I submit this list of ten commandments for husbands.

• Remember that thy wife is thy partner and not thy property. The wedding certificate is not a warranty deed but a working agreement. Any good wife who looks after the children and keeps the home in order earns half the income whether she works outside the home or not. It is said that marriage is a 50-50 proposition but a lot of people spent their married life arguing over who gets the hyphen.

• Thou shalt continue thy days of courtship forever. Usually the honeymoon is over entirely too quickly. Nothing is so powerful as flattery and words of praise. Little gifts pay big dividends.

• Thou shalt make as generous an arrangement in regard to money as possible. A wife asked her husband, "May I have a little money?" "Yes" he said, "how little?"

• Thou shalt neither criticize nor allow criticism of thy wife in public.

• Thou shalt remember the virtue of cleanliness and good appearance.

• Thou shalt enter thy home with cheerfulness. Cultivate a cheerful disposition. Be able to laugh at yourself.

• Thou shalt make thy home thy chief business. Let no business or club rob you of the time you should spend with your family. The family that plays together stays together.

• Thou shalt assist thy wife in establishing family discipline. Rearing children is a dual responsibility. Don't make it a duel. Agree on the rules for the children and stick by them as a team.

• Thou shalt remember the single standard of virtue and fidelity. There is one God and one standard—not two.

• Thou shalt remember thy Creator and seek to influence the members of thy family by precept and example for righteousness.

HAVING NEGATIVE ATTITUDE HELPS COMMUNISM

In case you are interested, here are 10 ways to help the communists:

1. Be suspicious of your leaders in church and state. If you do not like what they are doing just call them communists.

2. Talk down the church. That is what they have been doing in Russia for the past 50 years. The charming tourist guides will gladly take you to their churches and refer to them as "museums of antiquity."

3. Criticize our public schools and teachers. Spread rumors that the textbooks are slanted toward the communist ideology. Take one phrase of the book out of context and beat the author over the head with it as long as you have someone who will listen.

4. Quarrel with your neighbors. Be especially suspicious of those who may have an ethnological background different from your own. Become a divisive factor in the home, the church and the community. Communism thrives on factional fights. Divide and conquer is the communist motto.

5. Be continuously critical of your government. Assume that everything coming out of Washington is hogwash. Fool the tax collector every chance you get.

6. Believe all the bad news you hear. Tell everyone about it wherever you go. Pessimism and distrust is food for the communists.

7. Refuse to support the church and its related institutions. Someone has said they are leftist and most of the ministers are either "pink" or "red." Out of every dollar you put in the collection plate it is possible that one tenth of a penny will go to feed a child of communist parents.

8. Question all the good news you read about in the newspapers. In all probability someone is trying to trick you.

9. Renounce your faith in the United Nations, which was in large part established by the United States. The communists are gradually taking it over in order to establish communism throughout the world.

10. Deny the power of the spiritual. Trust only in the material. God is a myth. Might rather than right will ultimately win.

A SIMPLE MESSAGE, A COMPLEX MEDIUM

A popular preacher once said of his pulpit effort, "I always roar when I have nothing to say."—Anonymous

It is in vain for the preacher to hope to please all alike. Let a man stand with his face in what direction he will, he must necessarily turn his back on half the world.—Anonymous.

Preaching is truth revealed through personality.—Phillips Brooks.

To love to preach is one thing; to love those to whom we preach is quite another.—Richard Cecil.

The Christian messenger cannot think too highly of his prince, or too humbly of himself.—Charles C. Colton.

I venerate the man whose heart is warm, whose hands are pure, whose doctrine and whose life exhibit lucid proof that he is honest in the sacred cause.—William Cowper.

I repeat, you cannot have a live church with clergyman who is devoid of humor or dramatics.—George W. Crane.

Preaching is a personal counseling on a group scale.—Harry Emerson Fosdick.

It is no use walking anywhere unless we preach as we walk.—St. Francis of Assisi.

The test of a preacher is that his congregation goes away saying, not what a lovely sermon, but, I will do something!—St. Francis de Sales.

The preacher must have the heart of a lion, the skin of a hippopotamus, the agility of a greyhound, the patience of a donkey, the wisdom of an elephant, the industry of an ant, and as many lives as a cat.—Edgar DeWitt Jones.

Theological preaching is deservedly unpopular if all it does is settle a lot of problems people have never heard of, and asks a lot of questions nobody ever asks.—Robert J. McCracken.

Preach not because you have to say something but because you have something to say.—Richard Whately.

WHEN VIRTUE BECOMES A VICE

In the Protestant Cathedral, Washington, D.C., there is a group of sculptured figurines representing the seven deadly sins. They are pride, envy, anger, covetousness, gluttony, lust and sloth. Yet it is true that almost any virtue, pushed to the extreme and without love, can become a vice.

Consider the Pharisees in Jesus' day. They were men of prodigious virtue—obedient, conscientious, patriotic. Yet Jesus referred to them as a generation of vipers because they lacked love.

Consider the virtue of patience. Great victories have been won in the field of art, science, literature, music, character—all the result of infinite patience. Yet patience becomes a vice when we tolerate the things that should stir our moral indignation. If we are patient about civil wrongs, brazen injustice, and the like, then patience becomes a deadly sin.

Consider the virtue of loyalty, one of the finest words in any language. Nevertheless, blind loyalty to some of the ancient traditions of the church could mean the death of the church. Yet loyalty to the spirit of the living Christ can mean the renewal of the church.

Think of the noble virtue of patriotism. I have little use for the person who shows no devotion to the nation that nurtured him. But a fanatical patriotism can become a deadly vice. Those who were fanatically patriotic to Hitler's Germany 40 years ago must be held responsible for the slaughter of six million Jews and the death of untold numbers of soldiers. Wise old Samuel Johnson said, "Patriotism is the last refuge of a scoundrel."

Or consider the virtue of thrift. Some of the people I have met evidently believed that thrift was the only virtue mentioned in the Holy Writ. They spend a lifetime saving for a rainy day, evidently expecting a flood. But when the thrift gets out of hand, it chills the spirit of benevolence and human kindness.

Now consider the virtue of piety. I must confess I am uncomfortable in the presence of so-called pious people. They want to withdraw from the world and live a holier-than-thou life. Well, Jesus did not withdraw. He said, "Go ye into the world, preach, heal. . . "

True religion is evidently keeping one's heart clean and one's hands dirty in human services.

SQUARES SHOULD STAND UP AND BE COUNTED

Said one teenager to another, "Come on, chicken, don't be a square all your life." The word "square" is considered by some to be a dirty word which has gone the way of such other good old fashioned words as "modesty" and "patriotism." It is a word to be snickered over or laughed out of court.

I like the word myself. I can think of no higher compliment paid to any man than to say of him that he is a "square shooter." And when I must take another man's advice concerning the purchase of a used car or TV I am surely grateful for a "square deal."

A square is a person who rolls up his sleeves and goes to work at the job he has and refuses to wait for the "ideal" position. He is a guy who gets his kicks from trying to do his job better than anyone else. He is so lost in his work that he has to be reminded to go home.

A square is a guy who lives within his means regardless of the Joneses across the street and thinks that Uncle Sam ought to do the same. He is likely to save money for a rainy day and not count on his neighbors or Washington in a tight.

A square is a guy who tells his son it is more important to play fair than to win dishonestly.

A square is a guy who honors his father and his mother—and his neighbors next door.

A square is a guy who reads his Bible when no one is watching and prays when no one is listening.

A square is a guy who gets all choked up when the band plays the Star-Spangled Banner and when the flag is unfurled.

The pages of history are filled with squares such as George Washington, Abraham Lincoln, Ike Eisenhower—and the grandparents of some of us.

All you guys who believe in the squares such as these, stand up and be counted.

MARKS OF AN EDUCATED MAN

With high school and college commencements in full swing, what do you suppose are the marks of an educated man? Here is my idea.

An educated man keeps his mind open, and his mouth shut, on the pertinent issues until all the evidence is in. He will not jump at conclusions or make premature judgments. He will welcome any new evidence regardless of the source if it will lead him to the truth. Indeed, the educated man spends his life in pursuit of truth.

The educated man always gives a listening ear to the man who knows. Since he has two ears and two eyes he does twice as much listening and looking as he does talking. A charming young college sophomore was seated at a social function beside a young professor of astronomy. To make conversation the college student asked, "What do you study?" He replied, "I study astronomy." "My word," she said, "I finished astronomy last year." Imagine anyone finishing astronomy!

The educated man knows the value of the disciplines of life. He disciplines his mind because the more he disciplines his mind the better the mind will work for him. He disciplines his spirit by maintaining a wholesome optimistic attitude to life. Having the proper frame of mind helps him greatly in "having a good day."

The educated man plans well the course of the future. It is not hard times that wreck businesses so much as failure to call in expert advice at the proper time. "It is not surgery that kills people," said Dr. William Mayo, "but delayed surgery."

The educated man has worthy goals in life and relentlessly pursues his course to the end. He is aware that the greatest values are not simply material but spiritual. He knows that the essence of all learning is to give life meaning and purpose. He successfully relates himself to the whole of his environment . . . himself . . . his fellowmen . . . infinity.

OLD-TIME RELIGION

The chief trouble with the "Old-Time Religion" is that it is not old enough. We sing with zest: "Give me that old-time religion, It was good enough for Moses, It was good enough for father, And it's good enough for me." But that for which we clamor, beyond an emotional outlet, is not as old as we think. Our minds go back to the carefree days of childhood, our love for our parents, grandparents and the good old days that were actually not quite that good. If we really want the old time religion—and nothing is more needed today—we must be sure we get it old enough.

To begin, sighing for the religion of yesterday is a delusion. To be sure, religion ought to be old. The sun which makes for life on earth, was not made yesterday. The mountains, to which we flee in summer, were not a twentieth century product. Extreme fundamentalists who regard any interpretation of Christ more liberal than their own, seem less concerned over the advancement of the Kingdom than seeking converts of their own point of view. They remind me of the elderly lady who insisted we get back to the "King James version of the Bible just like God wrote it." Since God is Spirit, (Gen. 1:2) having no hands, such a feat would be difficult.

Religion which is really old is not a perpetuation of the dead forms of yesteryears. It constantly pioneers for God in new fields of labor. Abraham created religious history when he moved from Cana to the Holy Land where, through the prophets, the utterly reckless Jesus of Nazareth proclaimed "Ye have heard it said . . . but I say unto you." Nor was the old-time religion good enough for Moses. His revolutionary conviction prompted him to stand before Pharaoh and cry "Let my people go."

So we come to where every sermon should find its resting place . . . at the feet of Jesus. The old-time religion is the religion of Jesus . . . not simply a faith that will get us to heaven . . .

but one that will empower us to look forward, help the helpless, feed the starving, minister to the needs of all of God's children everywhere.

EFFECTIVE MINISTERS

The most effective ministers I have known are those who God has called. He (or she) is the best minister who follows his own advice.

Every minister, when he is preaching, should remember that God is one of his hearers.

The great preachers of the world are not the men who master their messages, but the men who are mastered by their messages.

It takes more religion to preach to one person than to a multitude.

The best theology is the fruit of kneeology.

There is no pulpit so vacant as the one without the message of the Love of God.

There is a vast difference between having something to say and having to say something.

If people sleep during the sermon the minister needs to be awakened.

The best education possible is essential; but there are ministers who are dying by "degrees."

Some ministers with doctoral degrees do not seem to have learned the alphabet in the school of Christ.

There are two fools in the pulpit: one who will take nothing from anybody, and the other will take everything from everybody.

There are ministers who will not heed the snap of a man's finger, but will give complete attention to the snap of his pocketbook.

Some ministers lambast the people because they do not pay more, when the people feel they are paying more than they are getting.

Some ministers have a wealth of thought; others have a thought for wealth.

When persons enter Christian work for money, there is the devil to pay.

Sermons are like bread—delicious when fresh; but when a month old, hard to cut, harder to eat and hardest to digest.

Ministers should not only have a smooth train of thought but also a terminal.

A sermon need not be eternal to be immortal.

FOUR THINGS

Remember the poem of Henry Van Dyke with these familiar lines?

> *Four things a man must learn to do,*
> *If he would make his record true;*
> *To think without confusion clearly,*
> *To love his fellowmen sincerely,*
> *To act from honest motives purely,*
> *To trust in God and heaven securely.*

To think without confusion clearly. Someone has aptly said that 10 percent of the people think while the other 90 percent would rather die than think. Most of us think with our emotions rather than our reasoning processes. We read those articles that confirm us in our prejudices; we pay scant attention to the arguments of the opposition. Basic problems are seldom solved by people with hot heads and cold hearts; rather by those with warm hearts and cool heads.

To love his fellowmen sincerely. We usually think of love as something like the love of a man for his blood brother, his wife or his children. We only complicate the issue when we think we can love every man on earth in this fashion. Some people are beyond our capacity to love. But we can respect them, honor them as potential sons of God, treat them as human beings. I understand we have tons of surplus products such as wheat and cotton in our warehouses. But there is a world shortage of good will almost everywhere one looks. We have polarized our hates and have assumed our chief adversaries were fellow citizens of the United States. Is this really one nation?

To act from honest motives purely. Homes have been wrecked, businesses have gone bankrupt, communities have been divided, nations have been arrayed in battle against each other because of the lack of common honesty. George Washington said he couldn't tell a lie, but some of his spiritual descendants don't seem to be able to do anything else.

To trust in God and heaven securely. Those who believe in a Supreme Being insist that He whom we call God is the norm of truth. In case of Russia, their god is the government. The government, not conscience, is spokesman for the right. And ours is a nation, under God, the God to whom we refer in our sacred state documents as Creator. Ours is a pluralistic society. We have no right to insist that all people fall down and worship our God. But our forefathers were monotheists. They believed in God and led, in the main, God-fearing lives. And the strength of any nation is the measure of the moral stature of her people. Oliver Goldsmith said it like this:

Ill fares the land, to hastening ills a prey,
Where wealth accumulates, and men decay.

SLOT-MACHINE RELIGION

There seems to be no end to the cheap, crackpot schemes calculated to make men rich. Some of these schemes are promoted in the name of religion. It brings to mind a slot-machine transaction: tithe and improve your financial status; pay five dollars to the church and expect a miracle next week; sow seeds of helpfulness and affluence will come back to you.

It is a cheap slot-machine religion when God is used as a means to an end rather than an end in Himself. Would you like to have peace of mind? Try religion. Would you like to have better relationships with other people? Try religion. Would you like to have a more healthy body? Try religion. A fatter salary check? Try religion.

Don't misunderstand me. Commitment to the ways of God may mean all these things. But religious faith is not a means to anything but the presence of God Himself. We seek God, not for what we get out of Him but for what His presence does with and in us. It is not a matter of using God, but a matter of being used by God. Salvation is not getting God on our side; it is getting on God's side.

It is a slot-machine religion when religion is reduced to a magical concept rather than a mystical experience. The more people rely on magic the less faith they put in mystical Presence of the Unseen. To touch a sacred stone, to stand in a sacred place or to repeat some sacred words, do not, in themselves, prepare a person for a spiritual blessing. The greatest miracles that are happening today are not in the realm of the physical but in the realm of the spiritual.

As citizens of the United States we pledge allegiance to the Constitution which upholds the spirit of democracy. But our salvation as a nation will never come to us through law alone. Paul spoke to us about "what the law cannot do." Liquor laws will not make us a sober people. Laws against murder and theft will not make us a Godly nation. Nor will joining the United Nations bring to us instant world peace. We are not redeemed by law but by the spirit of God in the hearts of men. There is nothing either automatic or cheap about being "one nation, under God . . ."

'SCARECROW' RELIGION FOR THE BIRDS

When I was a child, we had revival meetings in our church at least once a year. The visiting preacher had children's services for us in the afternoon after school was out. He invited all of us who wanted to go to heaven to come up and shake his hand. He said if we wanted to go to hell, all we had to do was to remain in our seats. Given those alternatives, we sprang out of our seats with enthusiasm.

Those were the days of hellfire and brimstone preaching. It is still being done today.

The Old Testament prophet Jeremiah refers to the worship of idols as being "like scarecrows in a cucumber field." (Jer. 10:5) Do you remember the scarecrows we had in the garden on the old farm? They were the grotesque, lifeless figures we put up to scare the crows out of the melon and tomato patch.

There is a type of Christianity that uses God as a scarecrow, which is as pagan as the idolatry upon which Jeremiah turned his scorn. Scarecrow religion is a perverted, distorted form of religion when it seeks to frighten children or adults into being good for no other reason that to avert the terrors of hell. That religion is as a scarecrow flopping in the wind when it is only a bunch of negatives and thou-shalt-nots. All the zeros in the world added together still make zero.

A positive Christian faith is expressed in a person's love for himself. He will not be a party to his own self-degradation. He will love his fellow human beings, regardless of race, creed or color, because he wants to be loved by them. He will love God because God made us in his likeness.

It is not the fear of God but the love of God that makes us Christlike.

In some of the books of the Old Testament, God is conceived as an angry war-god who leads his Hebrew people into victorious battles with their enemies. But the God represented in the carpenter of Nazareth evidently had no enemies. He only has adversaries. He allows himself to be killed rather than to kill. Is that not what Jesus said from the cross?

GOD SO LOVES ALL PEOPLE EQUALLY

What do you suppose are the five most meaningful words in English or any other language? It is my guess that they are found in the New Testament, John 3:16 . . . "God so loved the world."

Please note that it does not say God loved the white man more than the black man, the educated man in preference to the ignorant man, the rich man above the poor man, or even the good man in preference to the evil man.

Though there are hosts of human parents who desert their wayward children, it seems that God the father of mankind never, under any circumstances, deserts his children. He declares his love as universal and as everlasting as the stars above.

It happens, however, that we human beings desperately seek to make of God a partisan, prejudiced God. While God made us in his image, we insist on returning the compliment by desperately trying to make God into our image.

If we don't like the color of another man's skin we presume God doesn't either. If our religious beliefs differ from those of our neighbors next door, we have the audacity to assume that God is on our side . . . always.

Historians tell us that half of the wars recorded in history were religious wars. Millions of people have died trying to defend or capture the city of Jerusalem. Opposing forces thought of God as being on their side and they fought to their death.

Two opposing sects of the Moslem faith, the Shiites and the Sunnites, have been fighting across their borders for five years. The nations of Iran and Iraq have killed multiples of thousands of young men because they think God is on their side. It is said that Khomeini sees that all women in Iran taken in adultery are given the death sentence because he feels that it is God's will. Could it be that prejudice is our besetting sin?

During the Civil War, President Lincoln had a woman visitor who dropped into his office to give him a word of advice. She said, "Mr. Lincoln, I talked to God last night and he said he was on our side." The president replied, "Madam, I am not concerned about God being on our side; my only hope is that we are on God's side."

I think that God is neither Protestant nor Catholic, Jewish, Moslem, Hindu nor Buddhist. He is forever in love with all of his children. He has no enemies. He only has adversaries. His character is beautifully revealed in these five words: "God so loved the world."

'THERE CAME A WOMAN . . .'

There are two heroines in the New Testament whose portraits Jesus painted with unforgettable strokes of beauty. One was the poor widow who, when she went into the temple, gave all she had—two mites. The other was the woman of Bethany who anointed her Master's head with precious ointment.

On this Mother's Day, let us study this portrait of the woman of Bethany.

"As Jesus sat at meat, there came a woman having an alabaster box of ointment . . . She broke the box and poured it on His head."

"There came a woman." Think of the tremendous amount of history which is compressed in this phrase. There came a woman and Raphael, the artist, painted her beautiful face in the Sistine Madonna. There came a woman and Lord Bryon wrote the tenderest lines of literature:

Oh, when, my adored, in the tomb will they place me,
Since in life, love and friendship forever are fled?
If again in the mansion of death I embrace thee,
Perhaps they will leave unmolested the dead.

There came a woman whose name was Monica, and St. Augustine came into the world. There came a woman by the name of Nancy Hanks into a rough-hewed log house in the Midwest to be mother of Abraham Lincoln, and her grandeur was reflected in the life of her illustrious son.

"Having an alabaster box of ointment." Historians do not agree as to the worth of this ointment. In all probability it represented the savings of her lifetime. It was her most priceless possession. But it was none too good to anoint her Lord. She sought to give Him her very best.

Some people are quite content to give God life's leftovers of time, talent and money. Not this woman—nor any of the noble women of history.

"She broke the box." Consider the blessed ministry of broken things. Uncrushed quartz yields no gold. Unbruised flowers produce no perfumes. The broken things are often the most blessed.

Jenny Lind, Swedish nightingale, could never sing quite so beautifully until her own heart had been broken by an unrequited love. John Milton attained literary grandeur through eyes that could not see. John Bunyan wrote "Pilgrim's Progress" behind jail bars. Beethoven wrote the greatest music of his life after losing his hearing.

CHRISTIANITY IS A LOVE RELATIONSHIP

Christianity is to me a love relationship between myself and God as he is revealed in Jesus Christ. Differences in belief and the different ways of worshiping are minor matters in comparison to this love relationship. A man's denomination is practically always emotionally, rather than rationally, determined.

I am a Methodist, largely because of my devotion to my parents. Had I been brought up as a Baptist, Episcopalian or Catholic, I likely would have followed in my parents' footsteps.

The essence of Chrstianity—past, present and future—is loving Christ and the children of God. Since Christ held in complete loyalty the hearts of St. Francis, John Knox, John Calvin, John Wesley, General Booth, Pope John, Billy Graham and Albert Schweitzer, all of whom held irreconcilably different beliefs about him, I cannot believe that uniformity of belief is of prime importance.

The Apostle Peter became a Christian the moment he accepted the invitation of Christ to "follow me." In as much as Christianity is a relationship to the person of Christ, it seems that we seriously complicate matters when we insist that others are not Christians unless they believe as we do. Can we say: "Christianity is not so much in believing as in being?"

It is obvious that Peter, the first disciple, knew nothing about the Immaculate Conception, the Virgin Birth, the Holy Trinity or the inerrancy of the Old Testament. How can a matter be fundamental in a religion when the founder of the religion (Christ) never mentioned it?

I do not care to impress people with my theological concepts. I simply want to spend my life introducing people to him who said to his disciples "Come . . . follow me."

SLOW DOWN, LIVE LONGER

The prevailing American maladies are hypertension, anxiety and nervousness. Our doctors keep reminding us that living under continuous emotional stress brings about various kinds of illnesses; high blood pressure, heart disorders, arthritis, even the common cold.

A woman said to her doctor, "Please help me, I'm all run down." The doctor replied, "You are not run down. You are all wound up." For a definite reason the twentieth century has been dubbed the Aspirin Age, the Age of Anxiety, The Century of the Sleeping Pill.

What are some of the major causes of stress? For one thing, there is too much going on all the time. It is said that a typical Texan walked up to the ticket counter of the Dallas-Fort Worth airport and said, "Give me a ticket please." "Where to?" asked the salesperson.. "Anywhere," bellowed the Texan, "I've got business all over."

It seems that the primary requirement for membership in the Coronary Club is never to say no to any request that is made.

It is obvious that we are living at too fast a pace. I have heard people grumble because they did not get in the first section of the revolving door. Take a look at the many action verbs we use in the course of a day. We leap out of bed, gulp our coffee, bolt our food, dash down to town, hurry into the office, rush out for lunch, wade through appointments, whiz home . . . and often, unfortunately, suffer the consequences.

There is, as you know, a time change at the Texas-New Mexico border. A country bumpkin asked the clerk at an Amarillo bus station what time the next bus left for Tucumcari. "Six p.m.," said the clerk. "What time does it get to Tucumcari?" asked the stranger. "Six p.m.," said the clerk, "do you want a ticket?" "No sir," said the stranger, "but I would like to stay here long enough to see that bus take off."

Hard work seldom kills anyone. But anxiety, fear and worry is a real killer. If we quit running and settle down to an easy walk, the passing scenery will be more beautiful and the journey will be more enjoyable. That is the best way to postpone membership in the Coronary Club.

WHAT IS GOD'S LAST NAME?

A five-year-old girl once asked her preacher father. "Daddy, what's God's last name?" The father, swallowing a time or two, then, collecting his wits, said, "God's last name is . . . er . . .

Everywhere, honey. Everywhere." Not a bad last name for God at all. God Everywhere. God is spirit and His spirit pervades His creation in all of the areas of the universe.

The fact, however, that God is everywhere is not altogether satisfactory to some people. They want to know that the God who is everywhere is also somewhere, somewhere they can touch Him, feel His presence, discover the areas where He reveals Himself.

Let me speak as candidly as I can at this point. Through the ages, men have found God in His creation. If I want to know something about a writer I read his books; if a musician, I listen to his music; if a painter, I look at his paintings. The most significant miracles are not simply those recorded in the Old Testament, but those being revealed before our very eyes in creation today—a red rose growing out of the dark brown sod, a blade of grass on the lawn, the song of a mockingbird. Science can tell us how things grow from the soil. It does not tell us why. That great miracle is locked up in the heart of God.

Again, I find God on the judge's bench. As responsible human beings, we are responsible to the God who made us for the moral standards by which we live. I heard a man say recently that the conditions of the world were such that he had lost all hope. I haven't. The reason I have faith in the world and the people in it is because I believe in a moral God who demands of his people moral integrity.

The Ten Commandments on the part of many have only been broken, they have not been repealed. And men are still judged by the moral commandments of God. The Bible says, "Whatsoever a man soweth, that shall he also reap." This is true, not because it is found in the Bible but it is found in the Bible because it is everlastingly true. God is the judge of all men. He is still on the judge's bench.

In substance, God, through His Son Jesus Christ, is alive in the universe about us just in proportion to His real presence today in the hearts of those who love Him. A tough sergeant stood with an Army chaplain as he saw two of his buddies being wounded by a withering blast of enemy guns. With considerable cynicism the sergeant said to the chaplain, "Where is your God, Chappie, in a time like this?" A moment later two stretcher bearers braved the enemy fire, ran and picked up the wounded soldiers and brought them to the base hospital. "There" said the chaplain, "there goes God now."

"OUR"

You can tell much about a man by the way he uses the personal pronoun. If he is a consummate egotist he sprinkles his conversation with "I" "me" and "mine." If he is a cynic he frequently uses "they" and "their" . . . If he is an altruist his favorite word is "our" . . . one of the biggest words in the English language.

There are those who believe that "I," "me" and "mine" are natural while the word "our" is unnatural. But if selfishness is natural so is unselfishness; if egotism is natural, so is altruism. Even the animals show some degree of community. Bees swarm and ants live in colonies, dividing the work among them.

The word "our" ought to be more popular than it is. This is particularly true in the community of nations. When people talk to me about the failures of the United Nations I insist the failure is not in the organization, as such; it is in the selfishness of the member nations composing it. If and when world peace comes, it must be through some such organization as the U.N. As a family of nations we would get along much better if we used "our" more often . . . our world, our exploding population problem, our problem of ecology, the problem of our poor.

Good citizenship is expressed in that little word "our." It is our nation, and the more than two hundred million people within our borders are our fellow citizens whether we recognize it or not. The problems of the United States are the problems of all of the people of the United States. The crime problem is our problem; the problem of poverty is our problem; the problem of the use of drugs is our problem; stopping the war in Vietnam is not altogether an administration problem; since in the eyes of the people of the world we are all to blame for it, the war problem is our problem.

A more frequent use of the word "our" would save many homes now being threatened with destruction. If husbands and wives talked more about "our" children and "our" responsibility the homes of America would be more secure.

Because this word "our" is so important, I suppose that is the reason Jesus began the model prayer with the word "Our . . . Father . . ."

PRAYING IS MISUNDERSTOOD

George A. Buttrick, onetime Harvard theologian, once said, "Prayer is either the primary fact of the religious life or it is the world's worst delusion." Millions of people, having given up prayer, evidently conclude that prayer is a delusion. They are like children who pray for material blessings and when they don't get them they quit praying. Mark Twain's Huckleberry Finn had this experience. Huck said, "Miss Watson told me to pray every day and, whatever I asked for I would get. But it wasn't so. I tried it. Once I got a fishline but no hooks. It warn't any good to me without hooks. I tried for hooks three times but I couldn't make it work. So I sez to myself, there ain't nothing to it."

Others have said that prayer is irrelevant in a scientific age. Primitive man prayed that God might stay the ravage of disease. Modern man asks the doctor to inoculate him against the disease. Primitive man prayed to God for rain or to stop the floods. Modern man consults the meteorologist and builds a series of flood control dams. So why pray? Why not think—and work?

The misconceptions of prayer are legion. Prayer is not the practice of black magic. It is not cajoling God to dish out personal favors. It is not an effort to set aside the natural laws of the universe.

Prayer is communion with the Creator of the Universe. It is "the practice of the presence of God at the center of one's being." Prayer does not move the arm of God but it enables the arm of God to move us. Prayer does not ask for lighter loads but for stronger backs. He who prays is no longer alone in the universe; he is a welcome guest in God's house.

Elizabeth Barrett Browning said, "Every wish is like a prayer to God." A woman is praying when she is doing her best as wife and mother in the home. A man is praying when he is constantly practicing the golden rule in business. So Jesus said we should pray without ceasing.

True prayer is consecrated work. A student came into the laboratory where Louis Pasteur, the French scientist was hunched over his microscope, seeking to isolate disease germs. The student began a hasty retreat, saying, "I'm sorry, sir. I thought you were praying." Pasteur replied, "I am."

ELIMINATE YOUR RESENTMENTS

There is a story in the old Testament about two men who were employed by King Ahasuerus of Persia. (Esther 3). Haman was the Prime Minister while Mordecai held some minor office. Haman insisted that all persons in his presence should bow before him. Mordecai, a Jew, refused to bow to any one but God.

Haman became so resentful that he influenced the King to issue a decree condemning to death all Jews in the empire. He built a gallows on which he intended to hang Mordecai and his fellow Jews.

His plot was thwarted by Queen Esther, who also was Jewish. The King was so enraged by the plot that he ordered Haman to be hanged on the gallows that he had prepared for Mordecai.

Haman became the victim of his own resentment. There are many people who are victims of the same malady. They resent the person who strikes it rich, the fellow who drives a Mark IV rather than a Pinto, the one who gets the promotion ahead of him, the man who made unkind remarks about him when he was absent, and the woman who gossiped about her neighbor at the PTA meeting.

Resentment, if permitted to grow, actually will affect one's health. It is like poison in the blood stream. I shall never forget the comment of a doctor who said, "If he had only come to me six months earlier, his life could have been saved."

Even more serious is the fact that resentment separates us from God. It is impossible to live a Christlike life and hold bitter resentments against other people. One can't keep resentment and love in the heart at the same time.

If we do have such resentments, the only thing to do is to go to persons involved and make a clean breast of it. Hopefully, he or she will be conciliatory in attitude. If not, you have at least honestly tried to make amends.

Life is too short to carry on our backs a heavy load of grudges and resentments. We can get rid of them any day we choose to.

Someone chided Abraham Lincoln for freely forgiving his enemies. Lincoln replied, "My business is to get rid of all my enemies. I got rid of this one by turning him into a friend through forgiveness."

We can never forget that Jesus, God's human representative in the flesh, actually prayed for those who destroyed him. He would suggest that we go and do likewise.

DON'T BLAME THE MONKEYS

Human beings tend to blame our failures and weaknesses on something or someone other than ourselves. It begins early in life. A father scolds his son for pulling the cat's tail. The son replies, "I'm not pulling its tail; I was just holding on."

When the son trips his sister and she falls on her face, he absolves himself of all blame. "I didn't trip her, I just had my foot out and she ran into it." This tendency to point the accusing finger at someone else stays with us for life.

In recent years, science, without intending to, has provided people a perfect scapegoat for their faults by putting them in the category of the animal kingdom. The present controversy over the creation theory in the Book of Genesis and the evolutionary theory in the archaeological laboratories of the world does not bother me. I believe God is the creator of all living things and it scarcely matters if he took a minute or a billion years to bring to earth the family of mankind.

What does concern me is our sneering attitude toward God's first primate, the monkey. Every day I read stories about the atrocities of man that would make a monkey blush. How could they possibly feel complimented by our claims that we are distantly related?

The following is an imaginary conversation about the situation.

Three monkeys sat in a coconut tree, discussing things as they are said to be. Said one to the other: "Now listen, you two, there's rumors that can't be true. That man descends from our noble race; the very idea, it's a dire disgrace.

"No monkey ever deserted his wife, starved her baby and ruined her life. And you've never known another monkey to leave her babies to board with others. Another thing you'll never see, a monkey building a fence around a coconut tree, letting coconuts go to waste and forbidding other monkeys from tasting them.

"Another thing a monkey won't do—go out at night and get in a stew. Or use a gun, a club, or knife, to take some other monkey's life. Yes, man descends . . . But brother, he didn't descend from us."

BRAGGARTS HAVE SUBTLE WAYS

It's in the Book. Paul, in his famous thirteenth chapter of I Corinthians, said, "Love is not boastful." J. B. Phillips translates this passage, "Love is not anxious to impress."

When it comes to boasting, most of us don't use Horner's method of direct approach:

Little Jack Horner sat in a corner,
Eating his Christmas pie.
He put in his thumb and pulled out a plum,
And said, "What a good boy am I."

We are more subtle. The "conceited ass" is shunned like a plague. But there are many ways of boasting not easily detected by the naked ear.

There is the fellow who never enjoys a conversation unless he is the conversationalist. "That reminds me of a story," and he is off like a shot out of a cannon. You have to listen to some old tale, familiar to all of us since the days of Noah. He is trying to impress you that he is a first-rate raconteur. He never has any fun unless he has the floor fifty-five minutes out of every conversational hour.

Then there is the intellectual highbrow who looks with a jaundiced eye at the "dumb driven cattle" called the common herd. The only books worth reading are the ones he has read. The only conclusions worth holding are his own. He won't come out and admit that he is smarter than all the other people in the world. He simply arches a cynical eyebrow at all the opinions not expressed by his own divinely guided lips.

We must not forget the fellow who is positively certain that money and brains go together with love and marriage. He's in the chips and there must be a reason—his brains. He may overlook the fact that his father gave him a couple of million as a nest egg. He doesn't say he is brilliant—nothing as direct as that. He just reminds you of his three Cadillacs and his summer cottage in Michigan. His motto is, "If he's not in Dunn and Bradstreet, he's not in."

I hate to bring this up, but I've known preachers who were poor imitations of shrinking violets. All the time they are talking I get the impression they are asking themselves, "How am I doing?" Even Saint Paul admitted there were some things he didn't know. Some of Paul's fellow servants are not that humble.

The trouble with boastfulness is that it keeps one's self in the center of the picture. Pure, unselfish love goes out the window just in proportion as the desire to impress others comes in. If you jump in the lake to save a drowning child, you don't have to worry about making a beautiful swan dive. If you render aid in a highway accident, don't apply for a Congressional Medal of Honor. Don't bank on getting through Saint Peter's gates because you gave a pair of old shoes or a hat to the barefooted or bareheaded in Europe. Saint Peter just might hand them back to you . . . and make you wear them.

"Love is not boastful" . . . not anxious to impress.

LET YOUR FINGERS DO THE WALKING?

One of the most captivating ads in recent months has been the advertisement of the Yellow Pages. Two sets of fingers run up and down the pages and find what they are looking for as the persons let their "fingers do the walking" instead of their feet.

This is a good idea, within limits. But letting our "fingers do the walking" does not necessarily apply to the various aspects of the Christian faith. For instance, a few months ago a fine group of young people assembled in Dallas from all parts of the United States for services of testimony and singing in praise to God. It was a great tribute to this large assembly that policemen reported absolutely no disorder of any kind.

They came together to recognize the claim of God upon their lives. But they acknowledged the presence of God by the sign of a single uplifted finger toward the sky. We must remember, however, that God is not "out there" or "up there" but as Jesus said, "The Kingdom of Heaven is at hand," right here and now, no farther from any of us than the two steps of repentance and faith. In this case, faith, not fingers, does the walking.

We were all grateful that, during the Eisenhower administration the two words "under God" were added to the Pledge of Allegiance to the flag . . . "one nation, under God, with liberty and justice for all." But the fact remains that we cannot let our fingers write in these two words and make of this nation one which stands for liberty and justice for all men. We must put our feet in action and work for such a nation. Regardless of glib sayings of the politicians, equality of opportunity for all Americans is a figment of the imagination.

The denominational differences in America came about largely because of the disputes over the manner in which fingers do the walking through the pages of the New Testament. Given sufficient latitude we can pick out a dozen prooftexts at random and substantiate most any belief known to man. But if we use our feet to walk in "the way" as did the man of Galilee we stand on solid ground. We both defend and declare the Christian faith, not by tongues skilled in the art of argument but by feet dedicated to the art of service to others.

In no realm is the "finger doing the walking" more prominent than in the realm of prayer. We assume that all we have to do to call into action the mighty hand of God is to clasp our fingers in a prayer gesture and let God take it from there. But prayer is no lazy man's escape. It is reliance upon the co-operation of God amid the noblest efforts of man. God neither can nor will do for man what man has been admonished to do for himself. God is no cosmic bellboy to be commandeered to do your bidding. He gives you strength only as you seek to do (note the active verb) His bidding.

In one instance Jesus said to his disciples, "I am the way." He did not say by way of pointing his finger, "I know the way." He said he was the way because he had pursued it on foot . . . via Calvary and Easter.

LIVING UNDER PRESSURE

Everybody nowadays seems to be living under pressure. The businessman is living under the pressure of higher taxes and the fear of business instability. The lawyer lives under the pressure of keeping his practice ethical and his bills paid. The minister lives under the pressure of an overdemanding church and time to properly prepare himself for his sermons.

We should take heart in the fact that the great lives of history have been produced under pressure. An old proverb has it: "Where there is no anguish in the heart there is no music in the soul."

What made Abraham Lincoln great? Not his days of prosperity but his days of adversity. During his presidency brothers were fighting against brothers and, under such pressure, he furnished great leadership.

What made Jane Addams great? The challenge of the slums of the city of Chicago. It was the pressure of a sensitive conscience and the corruption of the city streets upon youth.

What made the writings of Robert Louis Stevenson great? It was because he wrote beautifully amid personal adversity. He said, "I was made for conflict, but fate has decreed that my battlefield shall be a bed and a medicine bottle."

What made Sir Winston Churchill a great person? Was it not because of the pressures he heroically endured while leader of the British empire during the dark days of the war?

Let's move on now to say that great Christian living comes through pressure. It never has been easy to live the Christian life. It never will be easy. Consider Paul, who admonished his followers to "endure hardness as good soldiers of Jesus Christ." Consider the early Christian martyrs. He who says it is easy to be a genuine Christian has never tried it. All who lift their faces to the sunlight of God must endure the fires of temptation.

How can you victoriously face life's terrific pressures? First, remind yourself that God has prepared you in advance to meet the strains of life. By God's help you can be master of circumstances—not be mastered by them. Second, you can conquer your problems if you face them squarely, one at a time. Finally, cultivate, in your quiet moments, the presence of God until He gives you the assurance of victory.

CATHOLICS AND NUCLEAR FREEZE

I have been very much impressed, as have others, by the stand of the Catholic clergy in support of the nuclear freeze. Since Catholicism throughout the world has a larger percentage of Christian believers than any other denomination, this position surely must demand our sincere attention. We can scarcely hope that Protestantism, as divided as it is, will ever be able to take a similar stand. It would simply mean even more divisions among us.

Though I am an outsider, it seems that Catholicism has made rapid strides forward since the days of medieval history. During the eleventh and twelfth centuries there were some half-dozen crusades wherein multiplied thousands of devout Catholics marched on foot from Western Europe in army fashion to capture Constantinople (now Istanbul) and Jerusalem from the Moslems.

They sought to use force to spread the word of God on earth. The most pitiful crusade was the one designed for children, most of whom were under twelve years of age.

In A.D. 1212 the children sought to capture the city of Jerusalem from the hands of the Moslems, but ignominiously failed at the expense of the loss of thousands of young lives. They have since learned that Christian people can advance the cause of Christ only through love . . . never through force.

One of the most effective novelists of the last century was a Russian by the name of Fedor Dostoevsky. In *The Grand Inquisitor*, Dostoevsky pictures the medieval church as a bone-crushing, arrogant institution void of love or mercy. The scene is laid in the Courtyard of the Cathedral in Seville, Spain.

The grand inquisitor is sent by the church to round up all the deviates and critics of the church and burn them on a bonfire in the presence of their families. Torquemada is the person in charge and he commands his men to cast the so-called infidels into the flames.

But at the height of the agony of the wives and children, says Dostoevsky, the Christ-figure moves across the cathedral portico, puts his arms around Torquemada and kisses his bloodless cheeks. To which Christ followers, Catholic and Protestant alike, now say:

"That's just like God."

FINDING GOD IN UNLIKELY PLACES

Where do you suppose people are most likely to find God in days like these? The poets tell us we usually find him in the things of beauty—the flowers, the sunrises and sunsets, and the twinkling stars on a summer evening.

This obviously is true, but sooner or later, if we find God at all, we must find him in unlikely places.

This was true of Moses, who grew up as the adopted son of Pharaoh's daughter in the lap of luxury. But when he saw an Egyptian taskmaster mercilessly beating a Hebrew slave, he became indignant, slew the taskmaster and had to flee into the Sinai desert for his life. It was while alone in the desert that Moses heard a divine voice saying, "The place whereon thou standest is holy ground."

While this is no excuse for murder, it is good evidence that the people of God need to be moved with indignation at the conditions under which some people are forced to live. When Jesus walked the streets of Jerusalem and saw little children being demeaned by their elders, he was "moved with indignation."

The apostle Paul who wrote the love chapter in First Corinthians also wrote "Be ye angry, and sin not."

Finding God in unlikely places is an everyday experience for many of our contemporaries. When Helen Keller, who was blind, deaf and dumb, wrote, "I thank God for my handicaps, for through them I have found myself, my work, and my God," she was revealing extraordinary insight. She found God in a dark cavern of silence.

A few months ago, Mother Teresa, the Carmelite nun of Calcutta, India, received the Nobel Peace Prize. Through the years, there has never been a more worthy recipient. She found God amid the stench and filth of the city where people were dying and no one else seemed to care. God was busy helping the people who were hurting and Mother Teresa wanted to help him.

A student in Union Seminary, New York made a trip one summer to the Far East and found his former professor, now retired, working in a soup line in an impoverished city. The student was shocked to see his former Greek professor, knee deep in filth, ladling soup for the poor.

"Professor" he said, "you are a distinguished translator of the New Testament what are you doing in that soup line?" His calm reply was, "I'm still translating the New Testament." He found God in a soup line.

CAN SCIENCE SAVE THE WORLD?

We err if we assume the Communists of the world are all atheists. They have a god . . . entirely different from our God. His name is Science . . . god of technological efficiency. The Communist leaders of the world are a forward looking people who work for and expect economic, social and political heaven on earth . . . through the god of Science.

The question is, can we hope for heaven on earth through the achievements of scientific and technological progress?

Science can give us a healthful world. There have been more "miracles" in scientific medicine in the last fifty years than in all past history. Science is simply the intelligent application of the laws of the universe to the needs of man.

Science can give us a comfortable world. Our air-conditioned homes, filled with electrical appliances are, without question, more comfortable than the palaces of the ancient kings. We are transported to the ends of the earth in complete comfort, and unheard-of convenience in the days of our fathers.

Science can give us a more intelligent, better informed world. By a turn of the TV dial we can occupy ringside seats and witness with our own eyes the significant events of the day. Proper distribution of the means of communication can conceivably solve the problems of mass education. Books by the millions on every conceivable subject known to man are available for the asking.

But can science save the world?

Never in history has there been greater production of palatable foods. Never in history has there been more malnutrition. The trouble is not lack of production but lack of distribution. This is a human, not a scientific problem.

Never in history has there been more dependable weapons of national defense. Never in history has there been more fear among the peoples on the earth. This is a problem of mutual faith, not a problem of science.

A man on horseback going to help a sick neighbor is a better symbol of progress than a supersonic plane with a bomb under its wing.

Science is amoral. The products of science can destroy us or befriend us. It depends on the character of the people who use them. This is a problem of human concern, not a problem of science.

There is something lacking in the makeup of those whose god is Science. The business of those who worship the true God is to put the "human" in humanity. Science cannot save us. "Thou shalt have no other gods before Me."

TAKE A LITTLE HONEY ALONG

"Take a little honey along," that's what the good book says (Gen. 43:11). There was a famine in Israel and food was scarce. Jacob, the patriarch, sent his sons down to Egypt to ask Pharaoh and his Prime Minister Joseph for a supply of corn to see them through. It was not intended as a bribe, rather a gesture of good will, when Jacob told his sons to "take a little honey along."

These are words of wisdom. Life is a rather grim affair and a little honey along the way is a welcome tonic. Honey means sweetness, gentleness, understanding, kindness. Blessed is the man who radiates the spirit of happiness and good will.

I have known a number of so-called saints in the church who, in my estimation, turned sour because they thought of life as a sentence to be served rather than an opportunity to be explored.

Someone said the reason Jesus associated with sinners was because he didn't like the surly disposition of the sour saints. While Jesus is remembered as a man of sorrows and acquainted with grief he was likewise a man of happiness and acquainted with laughter. The children loved Him. He had a great sense of humor. To become Godlike in one's life was, as far as Jesus was concerned, to be kind and generous to one's neighbors.

A woman of my acquaintance had the reputation of being a pessimist, a calamity howler, a personification of gloom itself. But one day I thought I noticed the faint glimmer of a smile. Taking my life in my hands I asked, "Are you happy, Mrs. Jones?" She grumpily replied, "I guess so." Then I said, "Why don't you notify your face?" Smiles, like colds, are catching.

You will have much more fun on your shopping tour if you use a little honey with the clerks who wait on you. You will enjoy your vacation more if you are determined to be kind to the filling station attendants, the waitresses and the other vacationers you meet. Take your clothes, your camera and your travelers checks along. But don't forget the honey.

Once upon a time, so the story goes, a doctor and his family toured in the jungles of Africa. They came upon a wild elephant that had been crippled by a heavy thorn in his foot. The doctor went to considerable trouble in removing the thorn from the foot. The scene changes. The elephant is brought to the United States to appear in a circus. As the elephant follows other pachyderms around the arena he spies the doctor in a cheap bleacher seat. The elephant stops, lifts the doctor out of the bleachers and relocates him in the reserved seat section. Not only do elephants have long memories, they believe kindness pays off.

WE CAN INCREASE OUR VALUES

Henry Wadsworth Longfellow could take a worthless sheet of paper, write a poem on it and make it worth from one to five thousand dollars. That is genius.

John D. Rockefeller could sign his name to a piece of paper and make it worth millions of dollars. That is capital.

Uncle Sam can take little pieces of green, treated paper, run them through the mint at Washington and make them worth one hundred or one thousand dollars. That is money.

A mechanic can take material worth five dollars and make an article worth fifty dollars. That is skill.

Picasso could take a canvas worth two dollars, paint a picture on it and make it worth ten thousand dollars. That is art.

God can take a seemingly worthless, indolent fellow, put His spirit in him and make him a blessing to all mankind. That is redemption.

There are very few poets like Longfellow. Most of us don't have the kind of brains he had.

The John D. Rockefellers are getting scarce, what with higher and higher taxes.

We have good mechanics, but competition is so keen in the industrial world that it is increasingly difficult to make a profit on a manufactured article.

We have hundreds of people who call themselves artists, but they are having a hard time painting five-thousand-dollar pictures on two-dollar canvases.

But there is not a man living who cannot increase his worth a thousand-fold simply by surrendering himself, wholly and completely, to the doing of the will of God. The word is commitment.

TO THINE OWN SELF BE TRUE

The above phrase is a quote from Shakespeare's Hamlet. "This above all: to thine own self be true. And it must follow as the night the day, thou canst not be false to any man."

The Bard of Avon was talking about the value of a worthy character. The worth of a man is determined not by what he has or by what he does but by what he is on the inside. If God were to speak to us in an audible voice he might say something like this: Be a worthy person. Stand on your own feet. Don't be pushed around by every passing fad. Live by an inward light. Be true to an inward loyalty. If skeptics divide the church, if vulgarity captures the social order, if the profit motive makes crooks out of the majority, if narrow nationalism blockades the road to world peace, have a conscience of your own. Let every man keep step to the music of a different drummer, however measured or far away.

In many instances there is a vast difference between a man's reputation and his character. Reputation is what you are supposed to be. Character is what you really are. Reputation is what you have when you come to a new community. Character is what you have when you go away. Reputation can be made in a moment. Character is built in a lifetime. Reputation grows like a mushroom. Character grows like an oak. Your reputation is what people say about you. Character is what you know yourself to be.

A Christian gentleman, used in its broadest sense, will be slow to lose patience but quick to forgive. He will not envy the good fortune of other people. He will refrain from trying to impress others with his own importance. He will have good manners. He will think the best, not the worst, of his fellowmen. He will not gloat over the wickedness of others. Above all else, a Christian gentleman will love his Maker with all his heart and his neighbor even as he loves himself.

The world as we see it offers us one of two freedoms. False freedom is where we are free to do what we like. True freedom is where we are free to do what we ought. The tragedy is that some of us have given first class loyalty to second class causes and these causes have betrayed us. The most beautiful element in the world today is the deeply committed life of a good person. One's real character is what he is and does in the dark.

JESUS LAUGHING

We have in our home a picture of Jesus laughing. I don't mean one with a faint smile on his face but one that expresses genuine, open-mouthed hilarity. It's interesting to note the reaction of friends who see it. Some actually appear shocked, some puzzled, other appreciative.

Why is this? We have seen pictures of great artist in art galleries where Jesus is being tried before Pilate, where he is carrying the cross, where he is hanging from the cross, and often forget the other 95 percent of the days of his life.

He was a human being who grew up in the Holy Land almost 20 centuries ago. He was a man of sorrows and acquainted with grief, but also a man of joy who was acquainted with laughter.

During the days of Jesus' ministry, he used humor in his open air sanctuary. To those who trusted in riches, he said, "It is easier for a camel to go through the eye of a needle than for a rich man to enter the Kingdom of God."

What is more awkward looking than a two-humped camel? What is similar to a needle's eye? See how ridiculous this comparison is. To the self-righteous Pharisees, Jesus said, "You blind guides, you strain at a gnat and swallow a camel." The Pharisees were very particular about their food. Imagine a gnat nose-diving into a cup of tea while allowing a camel to wiggle its two humps down the esophagus of those hypocritical of others.

Jesus pictured his critics as taking specks out of the eyes of other people while overlooking logs in their own. Proof of Jesus' humor is in the fact that great crowds, including children, followed him throughout his ministry.

Humor is the solvent for the grit of irritation that gets in the cogs of life. Those who can laugh at themselves and others will be among the last to have nervous breakdowns. Man is the only creature that God ever made who can laugh.

Paul, just before his own death, urged his followers to "Rejoice and again, I say rejoice." Amid the voices of pessimism today we dare not forget the lone voice of a man standing on the shores of a Galilean lake, with sorrow in his heart but with laughter in his eyes saying, "Be of good cheer. I have overcome the world."

The New Testament begins with the laughter of angels around the cradle of a child and ends with the *Hallelujah Chorus* sung by the saints of the centuries. Laugh and the world laughs with you. Weep and somebody steals your hankie.

CASTLE ON THE HILL

One of the most brilliant historians in 18th century Europe was a Frenchman named Voltaire. He still is being quoted, especially by politicians who remember his saying: "I don't believe a word you say but I will defend with my life your right to say it."

Another of his profound sayings was: "History is filled with the sound of silken slippers going downstairs and the thunder of wooden shoes coming up." Silken slippers represent the landed aristocracy leaving the castle on the hill and the wooden shoes indicate the economically disinherited moving in to take possession. Dip down in any period in history and see the living evidence of the continuous clash between silken slippers and wooden shoes.

Moses was the self-appointed leader of the first labor movement in history. Because of the Pharoah's injustice to the Hebrew people, Moses led them out to the land of promise.

A hungry mob in Paris stormed the gates of the palace of Marie Antoinette, crying, "We want bread." She contemptuously retorted, "Let them eat cake." And this was the launching pad of the French Revolution.

In the 20th century the clash of silken slippers and wooden shoes revealed itself in the advent of communism. Lennin's ideas captured the imagination of poverty stricken Russians, presenting a ray of hope for economic security.

I have seen thousands of poor Russians march through the Palace of the Czars gazing in wide-eyed wonder at the luxurious living quarters of their former tyrannical rulers. They are grateful that those palaces belong no longer to the few, but to the many.

The trouble with communism, however, is that while the Russian people pulled the Czars out of their hair they only exchanged them for a group of power hungry men in the Kremlin. If the common people don't like what they get, they are sent to Siberia . . . or destroyed . . . accidentally, of course.

We in the United States must forever keep in mind the importance of a three letter word ALL—a government of all the people by all the people for all the people.

MOONSTRUCK COUPLES MARRY

The most disturbing news item that I have recently read was the one of the mass-marriage of 4,148 young people into 2,074 couples in New York City's Madison Square Garden. The nuptials were performed by the Rev. Sun Myung Moon, imperial potentate of the Unification Church. The word unification is quite appropriate because no other man in history has ever before united more than 2,000 couples in 30 minutes.

The most astounding factor in the mass-marriage was that most of the couples had known each other for a short time, some less than a week. Some couples did not even speak the same language. And listen to this. Moon did the pairing-off of couples all by himself. I grew up thinking that marriage was the voluntary commitment of two young people of opposite sex in love with each other and making mutual vows of fidelity "until death do us part." It never occurred to me that two people could be locked into this highly personal situation solely by consent of the one performing the marriage. You talk about mind control . . . these young people were certainly Moonstruck!

Our priests, rabbis and clerics in these latter days obviously do not have perfect records in the field of marriage. There is one divorce for every three marriages, and the number is constantly rising. But we who perform our weddings in churches and snynagogues seldom fail to carefully counsel with newlyweds, often over a period of months. If God cannot hold a marriage together, it is ridiculous to assume that Sun Myung Moon can. He evidently thinks of himself as a latter-day messiah, robbing more than four thousand young people of their individual and rightful responsibilities to each other.

He had better get on with his messiahship lest the U.S. government succeeds in punishing him for income tax evasion. My prayers go out to young people who have been hypnotized by self-ordained false messiahs.

ON PRAYER IN PUBLIC SCHOOLS

With due respect to President Reagan and those who advocate an amendment asking for prayer in public schools, there are many good-intentioned people opposed to it. They are certainly not opposed to private prayer since they are among those who pray. But they are opposed to an amendment that would saddle the teacher with the responsibility of voicing a prayer suitable to pupils in the average classroom with so many divergent racial and religious backgrounds.

The real issue is organized, spoken prayers for groups of pupils subject to compulsory school attendance laws. Some of us feel this could be contradictory to the First Amendment: "Congress shall make no law respecting the establishment of religion, or prohibiting the free exercise thereof. . . . "

Prayer, properly understood, arises from the context of the person's particular faith. There must be at least a hundred religious groups in America with a membership of 50,000 on up. The children are expected, by law, to attend either a private or a public school. Their parents may be Buddhists, Hindus, Muslims, Jewish, Catholic, Protestant or whatever.

Is it possible that a written prayer offered by a teacher could express the sentiment of even half the students? A prayer, equally understood by all, would be so diluted as to be no prayer at all. Muslims, for instance, turn toward Mecca and prostrate themselves on the ground when they pray. No two people pray alike and no prefabricated prayer could hold the attention of all the students.

When religion speaks on the direct assistance of nervous politicians seeking a following, we have no right to call on our teachers to take upon themselves this added duty. It could make the situation more confusing than enlightening. Some polls indicate that more Americans favor prayers in school rather than church or home. How is that for parental irresponsibility?

OLIVER GOLDSMITH'S PHILOSOPHY

Oliver Goldsmith, the 18th century poet and novelist, once wrote:
"Ill fares the land,
To hastening ills a prey,
Whose wealth accumulates
And men decay."
It would be interesting to examine the meaning of this 200-year-old phrase in light of what is happening in the United States

today. Goldsmith evidently questioned the philosophy of his beloved England, whose chief interest seemed to have been the wealth of the nation rather than the well-being of the people, rich and poor, within the nation.

There is something wrong with the U.S. when 12 million people roam the streets looking for jobs that are not available; when good people, through no fault of their own, spend hours in breadlines to keep body and soul together.

In Goldsmith's day, honest hardworking people "decayed" because they gradually lost hope. It could happen to us here.

President Reagan has assumed, I believe honestly, that what is good for the rich will trickle down to help the poor. But it hasn't turned out that way, save from an elder Rockefeller to younger one.

America, boasting about its democratic ways, must be judged by the way it treats its minority groups. And these people are not being given a fair shake. Food stamps were taken away from some people who desperately needed them, simply because of a few grafters who muddied the water.

An inferior lunch was given poor children in our public schools because some people abused the privilege. Government loans to ambitious young people were curtailed because it was felt we needed additional neutron bombs.

Oliver Goldsmith was right. England, and every other country is wrong when it puts wealth ahead of people. A nation's people are the most important element in any community. Demean the people, especially the impoverished, and you ultimately destroy them. Dignify them, all of them, the rich and the poor, the strong and the weak, the blacks and the whites, and they rise to greater heights of expectancy. This is inevitably true because we were all created in the image of the Eternal.

THE PHILOSOPHY OF ABE LINCOLN

For years, Abraham Lincoln has been noted for his homespun wit and wisdom. Here are some of his sayings which speak to all of us. The first lines in each of the following paragraphs are his. My interpretation follows.

YOU CANNOT BRING ABOUT PROSPERITY BY DIS-COURAGING THRIFT. Buying only the things we need at the lowest figure is just good common sense. Thrift is basic in a free enterprise system.

• • •

YOU CANNOT HELP THE POOR BY DESTROYING THE RICH. Investments in business produce thousands of jobs for the common man. Both the rich and the poor and all in between are vital to our economy.

• • •

THE LEGITIMATE OBJECT OF GOVERNMENT IS TO DO FOR A COMMUNITY OF PEOPLE WHAT THEY CAN-NOT DO WELL FOR THEMSELVES. We all need to be supportive of our government but never insist that our government should support us except in times of obvious emergency.

• • •

AS I WOULD NOT BE A SLAVE, SO I WOULD NOT BE A MASTER. THIS EXPRESSES MY IDEA OF DEMOCRACY. Mr. Lincoln did for America what the Constitution called for . . . a government of all the people, by all the people and for all the people. No wonder that hosts of people throughout the world keep knocking at our doors for admission.

• • •

YOU CANNOT KEEP OUT OF TROUBLE BY SPENDING MORE THAN YOUR INCOME. Overextending one's credit, as a nation or as an individual, is creating havoc in today's economy.

• • •

YOU CANNOT FURTHER THE BROTHERHOOD OF MANKIND BY INCITING CLASS HATRED. We are a heterogeneous nation of all classes and colors. Sowing seeds of discord between groups constitutes a terrible disservice to the spirit of national unity.

• • •

YOU CANNOT BUILD CHARACTER BY TAKING AWAY A MAN'S INITIATIVE AND INDEPENDENCE. We must encourage self-assertiveness, independence, making our own way. In such efforts character is built.

• • •

YOU CANNOT HELP MEN PERMANENTLY BY DOING FOR THEM WHAT THEY SHOULD BE DOING FOR THEM-

SELVES. No able-bodied person should feel that his country owes him a living without working for it. Such a system will destroy the person and the country as well.

LAUGH AND THE WORLD LAUGHS WITH YOU

Everyone in the family, returning from church, complained about the services. Father didn't like the sermon, mother didn't like the choir. The teenage daughter said the pews were uncomfortable. The 10-year-old boy in the family said, "What did you expect for a dollar bill?"

• The minister was called in for the reading of the will of a wealthy businessman who had passed away. He and the many relatives were disappointed to hear the succinct contents of the will . . . "Being of sound mind and body, I spent it all."

• The minister told the church member who was delinquent in paying his pledge . . . "You are a good man and pay your debts to everyone else. Why don't you pay your debts to the Lord?"

"To tell the truth, preacher," the man said, "the Lord doesn't push me as hard as other people."

• "Were you a good little girl in church this morning?" the mother asked her daughter.

"Yes mother. A nice man offered me a big plate full of money and I said, 'No, thank you, sir.'"

• A church worker who was soliciting money for foreign missions approached the town skinflint. "I never give a dime for foreign missions," the miserly man said. The worker held out the bag he was using for contributions and said, "In that case, help yourself to some of this. It is for heathens anyway."

• A minister wrote to one of the world's richest men and asked for a donation to his church. The billionaire sent him a check for $10. "I don't know whether to cash it or frame it," said the discouraged clergyman.

• Billy Graham is reported to have received the following letter: "I admire you very much. I want to help in your worldwide crusade and am enclosing my check for $100. The reason I am not signing it is because I want to remain anonymous."

• An Internal Revenue agent phoned the local minister and said, "I am going over the return of one of your members. He lists a donation of $3,000 to the church. Can you tell me if he made this contribution?"

The minister said, "I don't have my records before me . . . but if he didn't, he will."

WHY BE A DODO?

All of my life I have heard that old-fashioned, out-of-date ideas were "as dead as a dodo." My dictionary tells me that a dodo is a flightless, gooselike bird, now extinct. Naturally I was shocked to find that dodo was originally the name of two men found in Biblical history. Since you may doubt my word, I will give you the references, Judges 10:1 and II Samuel 23:9 (RVS). Obviously I never met these gentlemen who lived some three thousand years ago. But if they were old foggies living with out of date ideas, I am quite sure I have met many of their descendants now living. The dodo bird may be extinct but the children of the Dodos are still with us. They, like the mythical whippenpoofel bird, always fly backward. They are not concerned about where they are going; they are only interested in where they have been.

The first sermon I ever heard on the radio was back in the '20s. A preacher from Zion, Ill., was insisting that the earth was flat and had four corners because the Bible said so. What else could the writers of the Old Testament say? They simply told the truth as they saw it. As late as the 17th century A.D. the church threatened to excommunicate Galileo, the Italian astronomer, because he insisted that the earth revolved on its axis making for night and day. Evidently the Dodo boys never sleep.

We have heard the quip "Times are not what they used to be." Well, in my estimation, they never were. We paint rosy pictures of the days of our forefathers, but I have no interest in repeating them. When I was a barefoot boy and had a cold, they put mustard plasters on my chest. Today I prefer an antibiotic. We talk about the old-time religion as being good enough for our fathers, therefore good enough for us. But our forefathers were victims of superstitions, witchcraft, racial discrimination, human slavery, etc. And when we hear people say we ought to get back to Jesus, we remember that he said in the Sermon on the Mount "You have heard it said you shall love your neighbor and hate your enemy; but I say love your enemies and pray for those who persecute you." Jesus is not back there with the Dodo boys. He is far ahead of us, the Man for all Seasons . . . and all centuries. So why be a Dodo?

IF THERE WERE NO CHRISTMAS

Have you ever tried to imagine what kind of a world it would be, had Christ never been born? Suppose there were no Christmas? There would be no churches. The skyline of the cities of western Europe and America would be drastically changed. Mosques, synagogues, shrines to be sure . . . but no churches, cathedrals. No spires, no crosses pointing skyward.

There probably would be very few hospitals for the poor and the indigent. Hospitals for the rich but none for the impoverished. There would be no leper colonies, for lepers are always poor.

There would be no orphanages for the world's neglected and abandoned children. There would be boarding schools for the children of the affluent but none for the poor, the waifs of the street, the outcast.

There would be many blank spaces on the walls of our art galleries. There would be no Raphael's Sistine Madonna; no madonnas of Murillo or Lippi. There would be no Hoffman's Christ in the Temple, no Holman Hunt's Light of the World, no Ruben's Descent from the Cross.

Our libraries throughout the world would be dreadfully impoverished. More books have been written about Jesus of Nazareth than that of any other person who ever lived.

The works of the great men of the world of literature such as Shakespeare, Tennyson and Browning would hardly be recognizable if the references to Christ were deleted.

Jesus never wrote a poem but he has been the inspiration of some of the greatest poetry in history. He never carved a statue, even in clay; but he has been the inspiration of the greatest sculptors through the ages. He had no school room in which to teach but he has become the great teacher of all time.

Had Christ not come the Bible would have been dreadfully incomplete. It would have ended with the book of Malachi. There would have been no words of assurance to give a departing companion such as "In my Father's house are many rooms." and "I am the resurrection and the life."

Quite probably the greatest words in the history of the Christian Church are these: "The word became flesh, and dwelt among us, full of grace and truth." Christmas means that in the fulness of time God came down from heaven with a baby on His arm.

HOW FAR TO BETHLEHEM?

When the shepherds of Judea, keeping watch over their flocks at night, saw the bright star over Bethlehem signaling the birth of Jesus they said: "Let us go over to Bethlehem and see this thing that has happened."

When we catch the meaningfulness of the advent of Jesus in human history we understand the importance of the question, "How far are you from Bethlehem?" We might put it another way: How far are you from the spirit of childhood? Are you teachable as a child? Or have you made up your mind and don't want to be confused by additional facts? Do you have the spirit of humility as a child? When we think of the power politics of the leading nations of the earth, including our own, we wonder what Jesus meant when he said, "Blessed are the meek for they shall inherit the earth." Do we really believe the meek inherit the earth? Politically speaking, the nations of the earth are living a considerable distance from Bethlehem.

How far are we, as individuals and as a nation, from the revolutionary teachings of Jesus? In the treatment of our adversaries, do we really believe in going the second mile, turning the other cheek, giving the cloak as well as the coat? This was a shocking statement in Jesus' day and it is a shocker today. Will the Christian spirit work in our kind of world? Has any great nation on earth ever adopted this policy? As G. K. Chesterton once said, "Christianity has never been tried and found wanting. It has been found difficult and not tried."

Years ago, when I was in college, a child some two years old wandered off from a suburban home and got lost in the woods. The police asked for volunteers to tramp through the woods and help find it. All night long we searched . . . hundreds of men and women. Then along about daylight, the piercing cry of a man filled the air, "We have found the child."

It will be a great day for the world when men of all nations move closer to the spirit of the Carpenter who was born in the city of Bethlehem. The chances are that most of us are farther from Bethlehem in terms of mind than we are in terms of miles.

MEET YOURSELF IN A.D. 2000

Years ago, I read a novel entitled *The Man Who Lost Himself*. It was pure fantasy, but it had one scene in which a lawman, age twenty-five, had been commissioned to locate a young fugitive from justice whom he believed was living in Paris.

In order not to arouse suspicion, he would ask the clerk in each hotel he visited, if so-and-so, giving his own name, had registered there. While the clerk was checking the list, he would glance down the registry, hopefully to find the name of the person for whom he was looking.

In one of the hotels he got the shock of his life. "Yes," said the clerk, giving the lawman's name. "He resides in room 313. The bellboy will show you to his room."

And when the lawman opened the door he found . . . himself . . . twenty years older and forty pounds heavier, but undeniably himself.

How would you like to open a door and gaze into your own eyes twenty years from now—say January 1 in A.D. 2000? This fantastic story can't be lightly dismissed because it has an element of truth in it.

Try to carefully analyze the direction in which you are now going. If you can scientifically predict the course of a missile as it leaves the launching pad, surely you can predict the nature of your personality twenty years hence.

Is your basic drive today money? You could wind up a Shylock exacting his pound of flesh. Are you interested in the problems of the people with whom you are associated each day? Or do you say you can't be bothered with other people's problems since you have enough of your own? You could end up with the reputation of a miserly Scrooge in Charles Dickens's *A Christmas Carol*.

Consider some of the habits we may have picked up along the way: throwing tantrums at breakfast because the coffee is cold; scolding the children for making noise when you have a headache; being part of a shady business deal. These habits grow considerably after twenty years of cultivation.

Do you really want to meet yourself upon the dawn of the twenty-first century? Let me make a simple suggestion. Just look at yourself in the mirror. If you don't like what you see, try making a New Year's resolution.

NOW . . . IN CONCLUSION . . . ON GROWING OLDER

In his poem, Rabbi Ben Ezra, Robert Browning wrote—
"Grow old along with me! The best is yet to be
The last of life, for which the first is made:
Our times are in His hands, who saith a whole I planned.
Youth shows but half, trust God. See all nor be afraid."
So, after careful consideration of the alternative, I have determined to stay alive as long as I live. One night several months ago, I went to sleep, conscious of the fact that I was in my late seventies and awakened with the startling realization that I had now become an octogenarian, living in the decade of the eighties. I discovered that old age doesn't slip up on us. It jumps. Since that time I have begun collecting a few aphorisms about the aging process. Here are a few of them.

Aging is—

When you know all the answers but no one asks you the questions.

When everything hurts, and what doesn't hurt, doesn't work.

When you feel like the morning after and you haven't been anywhere.

When your little black book contains names ending only in M.D.

When you get winded playing chess.

When the gleam in your eyes is the sun hitting your bifocals.

When your children start looking middle-aged.

When you look forward to a dull evening.

When your favorite part of the newspaper is "Twenty-five years ago today."

When you turn out the lights for economic rather than romatic reasons.

When you sit in a rocking chair and can't get it going.

When your knees buckle and your belt won't.

When you are 18 around the neck, 48 around the waist and 99 around the golf course.

When your back goes out more often than you do.

When your pacemaker makes the garage door go up when an attractive member of the opposite sex walks by.

When you have too much room in the house and not enough in the medicine cabinet.

When you sink your teeth into a juicy steak . . . and they stay there.

Since my last birthday I have been having more fun than ever before. And for several reasons. First, my wife has given up on reforming me. Second, I live without the pressure of writing a new sermon every seven days. Third, I have a good study at home and read what I wish to read. Fourth, I visit friends in hospitals on a regular basis. Fifth, I take a sufficient amount of exercise mornings and evenings. Old at eighty? I am having the time of my life.

—Gaston Foote